Beyond the Utopian Ideal

Beyond the Utopian Ideal

by Gary M. Douglas

ACCESS
CONSCIOUSNESS®
PUBLISHING

Beyond the Utopian Ideal

Copyright © 2014 by Gary M. Douglas

ISBN: 978-1-939261-46-5

Interior Design: Karin Kinsey

Published by Access Consciousness Publishing, LLC

www.accessconsciousnesspublishing.com

Printed in the United States of America

International printing in the U.K. and Australia

First Edition

WARNING

This is not a book you get through quickly. It's not light reading.

It's not a book you leave in the toilet.

This is a book you're going to have to study.

Don't buy it if you don't want to study and learn more.

Contents

INTRODUCTION

This book is the outgrowth of a seven-day Access Consciousness® event we hosted in New Zealand in the Spring of 2012. In the course of doing this event, I became aware that most people live from an ideal scene. They operate from a fixed idea or concept of how things are supposed to be rather than functioning in the moment, where they can change anything as needed to accomplish and create more. They spend their lives trying to create an end result of some kind rather than being in the generative moment of "What else is possible?" This creates a tremendous limitation.

We use conceptual constructs to create a purpose, a sense of rightness and a lot of other things that don't have to exist in our universe. Relationship, sex, sexuality, family and the future are examples of conceptual constructs. Society is a construct. Culture, religion and reputation are constructs. These things are not actually real; they are conceptual realities that have been dropped into our existence.

We buy into them, and then at some point, we give up our awareness in order to buy the rightness of this reality. We accept the notion that being normal, average and real—just like everybody else—is the best and only way to be. We alter our own reality so we can exist within a structure of the constructs we have taken on, where everything is supposed to look a certain way.

The problem with conceptual constructs is that they put you into conflict with yourself at every turn. Wherever you feel conflicted with yourself, you have gone into a construct. You're trying to do or be something a construct dictates rather than being you.

This book is about becoming aware of the ideal concepts and constructs that create limitations and barriers to what is possible for you. The constructs have to come off before you can truly be you. They have to come off so you can embrace total consciousness in a different way. They have to come off so you can create a world that works for you.

THE GOLDEN PLANET

I am writing a history—although some people might call it a novel—about the way ideal constructs came into existence. It's called *The Golden Planet*. On the Golden Planet, there was a sense of communion that doesn't exist here on planet Earth. We had a total sense of oneness with every molecular structure that existed. We had no technology. We had no cars, we had no motors; we had none of that because those things weren't necessary. If we wanted something to show up at our house, we didn't have to go out to get it; it would just show up at our house.

One day some techies arrived from a planet called Utopia. The techies had some flashy technology and created the image that they had it all together. We began to see them as greater than ourselves because they had spaceships. We had never considered the idea of going to other planets because we were having too much fun where we were. And if we had wished to be on another planet, we could have simply been there, without the need of a spaceship.

But because the techies were doing things we had never even considered, we began to see them as gods, and we began to adopt their points of view. Thus began a shift from being in oneness and communion with every molecular structure in existence, to buying into the techies' utopian ideals or constructs. We bought into the notion that ideals were going to take us beyond the communion and the oneness we already had. But a utopian ideal has nothing to do with what is. It's a construct, an idea; it's a substitute for true awareness and true communion.

In the end, we gave up oneness and consciousness for utopian ideals. We valued what we didn't have. We didn't value oneness and consciousness because oneness and consciousness were what we had. That's the way we get trapped all the time—by valuing what we don't have. This is how conceptual constructs are working in our lives today, and how we end up destroying ourselves and never getting what we truly desire.

(I've included the first three chapters *The Golden Planet* at the end of this book in the hope it might inspire you to see what it would be like to live without conceptual constructs.)

Since the time of the Golden Planet, people in all different times and places have bought into utopian ideals. Mankind has been seeking ideals for thousands of years. We have bought into ideals of economic, political and social perfection, some called *freedom*, some called *equality*, some called *justice*. They're all utopian ideals. We have created religions. We have written books about utopias and created utopian communities. We have become reformers of human society.

Socialism is a utopia, *capitalism* is a utopia, *communism* is a utopia, *democracy* is a utopia, *autocracy* is a utopia and *dictatorship* is a utopia. Hitler's point of view was a utopian ideal. Mussolini's vision was a utopian ideal. None of them are true, none of them are real and none of them work.

In the 1960s and 1970s in the U.S., *hippie communes* were an ideal scene in which there was (supposedly) no competition. There was no personal property; everything belonged to everyone. People didn't steal from one another. They just took your stuff if they wanted it—but that wasn't stealing.

The ideal of a *family* that will love and support you forever is another utopian ideal. Family is everything, family will always stand behind you, family will always be there for you. My ex-wife went to see her father as he was dying. He was in a coma. As she sat down next to him, hoping to have some final sense of communion with him, he opened his eyes, looked at her, said, "You've always been damn strange," and then he died.

Then there is the ideal of the *body* as the airbrushed image we see all over the place in magazines, TV, movies and the Internet. It isn't a real body; it has been altered to look perfect—but that doesn't matter. That's what is considered beautiful. It's the utopian ideal.

If you think the ideal body is supposed to look a certain way, you are compelled to judge your body. You compare your body to the ideal. Does that give you choice with your body? Do those ideal-ized images assist you to be in communication and oneness with your body? Or do they separate you from your body and invite and incite you to judge the hell out of it? An ideal separates you from what is real and causes you to judge it against your construct. And in the process of judging, your body becomes the judgment you put on it, whether it's old or fat or ugly or whatever you have judged it to be.

This is how the concepts are working in our lives today; this is how we end up destroying ourselves and never getting what we truly desire. A conceptual construct is a separation from oneness. It's the source of the creation of utopian possibility, as though utopia is greater than oneness. Crazy, isn't it? These concepts were dropped into your reality when you were a tadpole in your mother's stom-ach. You were told, "This is the way you are going to function. This is the way things work here. This is the only choice you have."

You may think that if you somehow reach utopia, everything will be ideal in all aspects of your life. You may believe you will end up with the ideal life and the ideal relationship. You will have the ideal business and the ideal amount of money. Everything will be abso-lute perfection. But that's not the way it works. Joyfulness comes in oneness, not in utopian realities.

Is your life better when you separate from oneness

and consciousness?

◊

BEING YOU

You have everything when you have you.

You Are the Gift You Refuse to Be

Before the techies arrived on the Golden Planet, we didn't hold onto anything—and we had everything. Then the techies came, and we bought the construct that holding onto things was going to make us something we weren't. I am talking about all the utopian ideals we've tried to create ourselves as. Say you've tried to create yourself as a cute, perky little blonde because that's what everyone around you believes the ideal woman is supposed to be. It's just a front or a façade you've created, but you start to believe it's true. Is that who you are? No. You are not just a cute, perky little blonde. You're not just a big, macho guy or a hotshot entrepreneur. You are the energy, space and consciousness that the infinite is.

Energy, space and consciousness are the elements of infiniteness. Everything other than energy, space and consciousness is a construct, not a reality. Infiniteness is not a construct; however, when we try to define it from a limited point of view, we create an illusion of what infiniteness is, that it isn't.

Are you attempting to define yourself as infinite? Or are you simply allowing yourself to be the energy, space and consciousness that infinite is? No boundaries, no limitations—just choice, question and possibility.

You've got to be willing to lose all the fronts you've created that aren't you, so you can be everything you can be as you, which is infinitely better than the fronts you've created as you. You have to honor who and what you are. You have to commit to you before you can receive you. You also have to commit to you before you can receive what everybody else is willing to gift to you.

Making a commitment to you is about the willingness to recognize what is true for you and to be that, whether anybody else goes for it or not. If you wish to lead a life without limitation, you have to make a commitment to living a life without limitation.

When you are being you, you are the invitation. When you're being you, regardless of anybody else's reality, people ask, "How come you can do that? How come you can be that? How come you get that? What is it you've got that I want?" When you are being you, you become the question. You become the curiosity. People want to know about you. You don't have to know about them because you already do.

Are you willing to commit to you, regardless of anything?

Persona vs Image

Persona is everything you are and that you will be, regardless of anybody else's reality.

Persona is real; it's alive. It's creation. It's a generative energy. When you're at persona, you have the ability to change and morph yourself into other things, but you, the personality, still exist. There's no pretense. It's just, "Here I am. If you like me, fine. If you don't like me, screw you."

Richard Branson is totally persona. He doesn't care about defining himself in a certain way. It's irrelevant to him. Hugh Jackman does persona. He's quirky, he's charming and he can change on a dime. That's what endears him to us. Brendan Fraser is another one. He can do anything and he can go anywhere because he presents different parts of his personality in each role that he does. He doesn't limit himself to, "I'm a cool guy" or "I'm a superhero." He can make fun of himself, he can do comedy, he can do the whole bit. As a result, his range is bigger.

Image is what you think you have to be. Image is a construct. It's the self you want everyone else to see you as. You create an image of how you want people to see you, and you live as though that image is you. That's who you have to be all the time. You try to look the way you want people to see you. When you do image, you're presenting a façade for people to look at. It's one-dimensional. You have to exist in a constant state of judgment of yourself because you're constantly trying to maintain your image. Let's say you decide to be extremely feminine. That's a construct. You think you have to do something in order to be feminine. What if you didn't have to prove you were feminine? What if you were just being you—and that was the ultimate in femininity?

Instead of being who we are, we put out an image of what we think we need to be to prove that we are whatever we think we're supposed to be. We try to show we are being something rather than actually being what we are.

Mitt Romney does image, and Obama has persona. He actually is a person. In the beginning of his career, Tom Cruise had persona too, and we felt connected to him, then somewhere along the line, he began to create an image of the way he wanted people to see him, and now we don't much care about him. Mel Gibson is another one who started doing image instead of persona. He used to be alive and exciting; now we look at him and say, "Uh, never mind." Madonna did persona for a long time. Now she is doing image as well. The same is true for Oprah. She was once a major personality. Now she's pushing herself into image.

When you do image, you present a pretense of who you are. Persona, on the other hand, gives you the opportunity to show different parts of you, the chameleon aspects of you. Image is never you. It's always a picture of who you want people to see you as. When you try to create you as the person you want to be seen as instead of who you are, you are dead.

Years ago, a lady said to me, "You're the most unmarried married man I have ever met. You are just you wherever you are. You don't talk about your family, you don't act like you're married, and you are just present as you."

I said, "Yeah, doesn't everybody do that?"

She said, "No."

It was a shock to me to discover that people would give up who they are in favor of who they are as a married person. That's doing image. It's a construct.

Image is an institutive energy rather than a creative energy. When people do image, they keep going to the same place and doing the same thing in order to get the same result. But that doesn't change the world and it doesn't create greater possibilities. People think their image is going to create them, but in truth, it handicaps them. The ability to create disappears when you go to image. You can't create from image.

When you get into conceptual constructs, you tend to lose you. Have you ever had the experience of losing you, especially in a relationship? When you are being you, something different starts to show up. Have you ever noticed? Look at times when you have had no sense of separation and no sense of need. There was no force, there were no requirements and no desires, just a willingness to enjoy the hell out of you. Then a man (or a woman) showed up and you gave it all up. When you're around other people and you notice that you're starting to give yourself up, try asking, "Would an infinite being truly choose this?"

How many illusions of who you are have you created in order to buy the idea that the illusion you created is the real you, so you won't have to see the real you that wouldn't match the illusion you've created of you—that would be something that you might not be able to control as well as the illusion?

Being What You Are in Every Respect

You have to get to the point where you say, "I don't care who I turn out to be. I want to know everything about me. I don't care if I lose everything and everyone. I want me. I have no clue who I am, because I have never chosen to see me, be me, want me, desire me or like me better than anybody else." You have to ask yourself, "How stupid am I not to choose to be me?"

Have you ever been encouraged to be you? No. You have been encouraged to do what other people want you to do, to live your life by other people's points of view and utopian ideals, and to do what everybody else says is right for you. No one has ever encouraged you to live as you and be all of you, no matter what that turns out to be.

Ninety-nine percent of the people on the Earth are not willing to see who they are because they have not been encouraged to be who they are. You may try to see other people for who they truly be; you may even try to get them to see themselves. Do they actually choose that? How often and how much? They see one tiny little bit of who they are, and that's all they're willing to see.

I was willing to look at myself and ask, "Okay, what am I? I am a killer." I know I was a killer because I did past life regressions. I saw where I did that. Then I asked, "So, I'm a killer. What else am I?" I saw where I was a psychic. I saw where I was brilliant. I saw where I was kind. I saw where I was a saint. I was willing to look at all of this and say, "Wow, I am so much more than I think I am."

You've got to be willing to be everything. If you realize you can be a thief and you are a thief, then you have total freedom to choose. It doesn't mean you have to go out and steal from people. It just means you are willing to be all that you are. If you have the point of view that you can't be a thief or you shouldn't be a thief, you are choosing from the menu of what is right. You're choosing from your construct of goodness, your construct of rightness and your construct of what you've decided you should be.

Once in a class in New Zealand, we were talking about the Maoris. I said the Maoris had a brilliant way of dealing with marriage. They would have a great celebration when they got married, then later, if the husband wished to end the marriage, he would say to the woman, "Go home to your mother." Or if the woman wished to end the marriage, she would say, "I am going home to my mother." That was the end of the relationship.

I said, "Can't we institute that, please?" No more courts and settlements. Just, "I'm going home. See you later." It is so simple.

A lady who was in the class said, "You're just one of those Maori lovers."

I said, "And the point is? What do you mean?"

She said, "It's disgusting that you love those black people."

I said, "You can only hate or have a judgment of anything that you have been or done. How many lifetimes were you a black person?" It was crazy. She was judging herself and creating separation from herself and the people around her. Her prejudiced points of view were creating tremendous limitations for herself and others.

When she finally admitted that she had been a Maori princess in another life, she was pissed that she wasn't a princess this lifetime as well. And she was pissed at the Maoris for not recognizing her as the princess she was.

So, what have you been or done that you don't want to acknowledge you've been or done, that if you acknowledged you've been or done it, would allow you more freedom?

What is it you're afraid to look at about you? Do you not want to see the good, the bad and the ugly? Are you only willing to see the good? Are you refusing to see the bad? Do you not want to receive the ugly?

Or are you refusing to see the good in you because as long as you're bad and ugly, you know you'll get what you want? A lot of people think this. They're not willing to see the kindness, the caring and the loving they are. They think that with those qualities, they won't be able to get everything they desire and they will be destroyed. Is that a truth or a lie? It's a lie.

If you're not willing to see that you're the smartest person on the planet or that you're one of the top one percent in the world in intelligence, then there's a part of you that you have never been willing to perceive or receive and you've definitely not been willing to be. Being and receiving go together. When you are willing to totally be you, you can receive everything. And because you can receive everything, your awareness expands. Your awareness will expand exponentially once you're willing to acknowledge who and what you are.

I'm not talking about stepping up to being you. You think stepping up means you're going to be something greater than what you are. That's not it at all. Don't try to be greater than you are. Just be what you are in every aspect.

How much more are you than you think you are,

that you are refusing to perceive, know, be and receive?

Choosing All of You

I have a friend who has an amazing way of looking at the world. Thank God she has an eye for beauty; otherwise, she wouldn't survive in this reality. She goes out, looks at a pile of toxic waste, makes it look pretty, and takes a picture of it. She says, "Look at the pretty toxic waste."

People say, "You touched that shit? You could be toxified forever."

She says, "Oh, but it looked so much better when I rearranged it."

When she was a kid, she heard her parents talking about her behind closed doors. They were trying to figure out what they were going to do with her because she was so weird. She didn't see what everybody else saw—she saw the insane beauty of the world.

She had an aunt who made all the kids in the family, twenty of them, bow down on the marble floor of a hotel in San Antonio and worship the virgin eye in the banister. The mother and the grandmother were saying, "Get up! Get up! That's insane!"

"No," the aunt said, "It must be so."

Her grandfather kept live rattlesnakes in the refrigerator. He said, "Well, when you cool them off, they get slow." One day when his wife was taking a nap, he found a little wild pig, brought it home, and turned it loose in the bedroom with her.

And once her son let off a smoke bomb outside the house and blue smoke went into her beautiful home through the bedroom window. Any parent would be cranky about that, but she said, "You should have seen all the different shades of blue!"

She did an art installation about black cowboys in America. Some people in Texas were horrified; they ripped, shredded and cut things up in the installation. Their point of view was, "How dare you say good things about black cowboys?" But she wasn't saying good things about them. She was simply trying to show their perspective. She does things like that.

There were some Latino people who came over from Mexico with a coyote. These people and their kids were left locked inside a truck on the side of a road in 150-degree heat with no water. They all died. She went out and photographed the teddy bears and things they left behind. The photos made me cry. People said, "How can she photograph this? I don't want to talk about this stuff. This stuff doesn't exist." For her, it not only exists; she sees the beauty in it and she sees the insanity in it. She sees the possibility and the question in it, and she doesn't come to conclusion.

I said to her, "You're thinking that because you don't come to conclusion that you're an airhead and you're wrong. You're a beautiful airhead, honey. You're insane. What's wrong with that? I am insane too, but I don't deny it."

She sees the world with a different eye. You've got to get that you have a way of seeing the world too. That's your eye; that's your reality. It's not wrong. It's not a mistake. The fact that you see the world through different eyes is not a badness. It's a goodness.

Stop trying to figure out what's wrong about you. If you're going to be you, you have total choice. If you're not going to be you, you don't. You've got to look at all the parts and pieces of you and not think any part is not acceptable or not allowable.

> What mistake are you not willing to make, that if you would make it, would give you all of you? Everything that is times a godzillion, will you destroy and uncreate it all? Right and wrong, good and bad, POC and POD, all 9, shorts, boys and beyonds.*

---

* "Right and wrong, good and bad, POC and POD, all 9, shorts, boys and beyonds" is the Access Consciousness® clearing statement.™ There is a brief explanation of what the words mean at the end of the book.

Do you want to live like other people—or do you want to change the world? You want to change the world. Would you please acknowledge and recognize that? Every morning when you get up, ask, "How do I change the world today?" You change the world by being you.

You've got to choose to be everything you are, regardless of whether anybody else goes along with it. If you don't, you're diminishing the possibilities that exist in the world. If you don't step up to everything you are, you're limiting you, you're limiting me and you're limiting everybody around you.

Do you have something to offer the world that you have not been willing to offer? What if you were willing to offer what you truly have to offer, that you've never been willing to be, know, perceive or receive?

Everything that doesn't allow you that gift to the world, will you destroy and uncreate it all? Right and wrong, good and bad, POC and POD, all 9, shorts, boys and beyonds.

What are you trying not to be that you actually are,

that if you would be it, would change all reality?

Change You—Change the World

We keep looking for a way to change the world to make it a better place. Do you truly believe all things can change? Is that real to you?

The one thing you can always change is you. You can't change other people. All you can do is be and do something different to change you. And changing you will change the people around you. You are a major component of the planet. What you do here has an effect over there. What you choose here has an effect on the other side of the world. What you change here changes everything and everyone around you, and different possibilities can show up based on you changing you. You're the only person you can truly change. You're the only person that you can truly control. And as you change, you change everybody around you.

You're the only person who can be who you truly be.

Consciousness is the antidote to utopian ideals. When you choose consciousness, your consciousness invades everything and everyone, and that, in turn, creates more consciousness. The more you choose consciousness, the more you will permeate other people's reality and the less they will be willing to hold on to their limitations. Your being conscious actualizes a different reality. You become a catalyst for change.

By being you,

you change everything and everyone around you.

Scan for more information

◊

LOSING YOUR CONSTRUCTS

As long as you are buying conceptual constructs and utopian ideals,

you cannot truly see what is.

Are You Willing to Give up Your Utopian Constructs?

An ideal is something that you have judged to be greater than what is. I never have an ideal scene that I'm looking for. I don't look for something to be greater than what is. I function from pragmatic choice, which means I deal with what is—with facts and observable occurrences rather than constructs and ideals. It's got to be practical. It's got to be something I can use. I ask, "How is this going to work? What is this going to look like? What is this going to lead to?" I look at, "What is it?" because what it is, is what it is.

Each person has one to seven utopian concepts that are the source for the way they create their life. The concepts are different for each person. To recognize your utopian concepts, you have to look at the areas of your life where you seem to disappear. If you start down a trail and you seem to fade away, you're on the way to a utopian ideal. You disappear out of the computation of your life as part of the payment for maintaining the illusion of what you're going to get if you keep going down the path after the utopian concept.

You have to contract dynamically in order to have a fixed point of view of any construct. It is viscerally abrasive. You feel it in your body. When I am around people who are doing a lot of contraction, I feel like I am being shot with darts or hit upside the head with a two-by-four. It's anything except space—and what we truly are is total space. Contraction didn't create the construct, and the construct didn't create the contraction. But to keep a construct in existence requires contraction.

As you start to break down the conceptual constructs, you begin to see what is—but as long as you are buying conceptual constructs, you cannot truly see what is. You only see what you have decided should be, what has to be or what ought to be. You only see what should happen that isn't happening. You are always looking for a way to make a conceptual construct an ideal scene, where you reach a state of nirvana, God or heaven. The conceptual construct is that everything will be as it is supposed to be as though there is a pre-ordained reality you're supposed to be living from. Uh-oh, there goes the utopian ideal of *destiny*.

Have you sold your awareness for the perpetration and

perpetuation of the promise of a utopian ideal?

Some of the most common conceptual constructs of this reality are *time, being right, the ideal scene, marriage, family, religion, self and higher self* and *money*. There's also *sex, relationship, power, bodies and embodiment, your group, your phylum, your kingdom, your species* and many others.

Time

Time is a conceptual construct you use to slow yourself down enough to fit into this reality. The construct of time slows you down to the point that you can't accomplish all the things you would like. If you were willing to lose the limitations of time, everything you did would happen with greater ease. If you lose time as a construct, if you lose time as something that's valuable to you, if you lose the value of time, space begins to fold and mutate around you so that you accomplish things in minutes that take everybody else days to do.

A friend asked me to help her with her mother's estate. Her mother had a two-bedroom condo stuffed with beautiful antiques. My friend and her husband had been at the mother's condo for four weekends and they had barely scratched the surface of dealing with what was there. I arrived at nine o'clock one morning and we began to go through things. By 11:30, we had gone through everything. I said, "Okay, now you need to call somebody to come and look at this stuff and we can set up a garage sale or see if somebody will take these things on consignment. Why don't we go to lunch?"

She could not believe that in two and a half hours, I had gone through everything. She and her husband had not been able to get through one room in eight days. That's my life. I can do things in two and a half hours that take other people ten days to accomplish. That is what it can be like if you don't try to create from the construct of time.

When you're willing to lose time as a construct of reality, when you don't attempt to make time real, it doesn't take time to accomplish things. I'm not interested in time. I'm interested in space. I always get to places on time without knowing what time it is. If you function from space, you have the capacity for *knowing*, which is very different from *thinking*. If you function from time, you have to function from thinking. But awareness comes from knowing, not from thinking about your experience. You think experience equals awareness. It doesn't. That's the idea that it takes time to be aware. Awareness can be instant.

Recently I was going to fly to Australia, and I needed to be at the airport in Los Angeles no later than 9:30 in the evening. My driver asked what time he should pick me up. I said, "How about 7:00?" He arrived at 6:45, we got my bags in the car and were out the door by 7:00. There was absolutely no traffic, so I got to the airport in an hour and a half, which never happens. I went up to the check-in counter, and the woman said, "Sir, your flight has been cancelled, but I have an opening in business class on an earlier flight." I had to go immediately to board the plane. Had I not arrived at the airport at 8:30, I would not have made the flight and I would have been stuck there for nine hours until the next scheduled flight.

Somehow I knew I had to leave home at 7:00. When I told the driver we needed to leave at 7:00, it was not based on a logical, linear universe or on a construct that had anything to do with anybody else's world. It was just an awareness or a knowing that I needed to leave at that time, even though logically speaking, it didn't make sense. I didn't try to figure it out or think it through: "It takes one and a half hours if there's no traffic, and two-plus hours if it's during rush hour. Therefore we should leave at such-and-such a time." Instead, I went with my awareness. I allowed the information I needed to be there.

Peace with time is knowing that you have to do something but not why you have to do it and then doing it without having a clue why you have to do it. I ask myself, "What do I know? What time do I need to go?" not "What time should I go according to the schedule of time on this planet?"

Time is a way you function in order to maintain the contraction of your awareness. Have you ever said, "I don't have enough time?" Does saying that expand your universe? Or does it contract your world and make you more frantic? You say, "I don't have enough time. Now I'm frantic. I have adrenaline pumping, so I know I am going to get something accomplished." You rev up the adrenaline, and then all of a sudden, you get very tired and you have to go to sleep. Do all the things you decided you didn't have time to accomplish get done? Nope.

Because I don't buy time as a construct, I can do all sorts of things other people struggle with. I can meet somebody for the first time and know everything about him or her in an instant. I don't have to spend time with people to know about them. I know it all instantaneously. I can practically tell them how many abortions or illegitimate children they have had. And I don't have any judgment or any point of view about the things I know. It's never an issue for me because I don't have a conviction about anything. My point of view is, whatever you choose, it's your choice.

Spending Time

Spending time is another construct related to time. People say, "We've spent so much time together" or "We spent a lot of time to create this." Nobody talks about being or caring or enjoying. No one says, "Wow, it was really fun to be with you." They say, "I spent so much time with you," as if that actually means something.

Have you ever been in a relationship where the person said to you, "We're not spending enough time together?" What is it you're spending in the relationship? Yourself. That's why, when a relationship is over, people get angry and say, "I spent the best years of my life with you." Well, if those were your best years, what's wrong with that? They're gone. But you're not really upset about the time you spent; you're upset that the person doesn't want to be with you any more.

Would you consider the possibility of losing the construct

of time as the creation of your life?

All People Are Good

At one time you may have adopted the conceptual construct of the utopian ideal reality that all people are good, so you always have to look for what's good about people. You don't want to see what is bad about them. When you do that, you can't see what's not going to work about them. You can't see where they're going to work against you. You can't see where they're going to be your enemy and not your friend.

Years ago, I was in real estate and I met a couple I decided were really good people. I put them into an apartment I was renting because they were going to take very good care of it and do well by it. When they moved out, there were feces on the wall and almost everything in the whole place was destroyed. The "good people" did bad things. This was the point where I saw that I had to look at more than what was "good" about people. I needed to see what they couldn't do as well, because if you don't look at what people can't be or can't do, you're putting on blinders to maintain the idea that everyone is good.

I know people who have good in them and I know people who have bad in them, so when I'm dealing with them, I ask what they are going to choose at any one time. I don't have the point of view that anyone is good or bad. That's because everyone is good and bad.

Would you consider losing the construct that all people

are good—and begin to see what is?

Being a Good Person

You have so many judgments about the utopian ideal of what *being a good person* is that you try to take the strengths of you and make them a wrongness. You say, "I will prove that I am the best person ever by doing x, y and z." That doesn't prove anything except that you are choosing the limitations you have decided will prove you are better than the judgments you have about what you are not good at. Every one of those utopian ideals is based on judgment. None of them is based on awareness.

I have a friend who is one of the kindest and most caring people I've ever known. She is always looking for the good in people. She will have the idea that another person is good, and for her, that means the other person is better than she is. She always sits in judgment of herself to determine how she can be as good as other people. She's in a constant state of comparison and contrast with what they're choosing, and if they choose something not good, she has to see herself as worse—not better—because she has already decided they are good.

Would you like to give up all your conceptual

constructs of good person, intellectual person,

intelligent person and perfect person?

If you do, you will create a new possibility for you

Being Right

Another common construct is *being right*. *Correct* and *right* are two different things. *Correct* is a level of awareness. It's when all things match. It's a recognition of what is: "The house is white." It's not right—but it's correct. *Right* is the necessity to judge. It is a position of authority. What makes you right and everybody else wrong? That's something you're definitely not willing to lose.

I worked with a lady recently who asked me to tell her what she wasn't willing to see. I said, "What you don't want to see is that you have a necessity to always be right."

She said, "Well, of course, because if I'm wrong, I disintegrate and disappear."

I asked, "How much judgment do you have to do to prove that you are right? And how much awareness do you have to cut off to maintain your rightness? And how much are you willing to receive from others that would contribute to your life if you are only right? If you have to be right, you can't receive contribution. You can only reject people and what they have to give you."

She almost fell apart on me. She looked at it for days, and said, "Oh my God, I never realized—I didn't know that I had such a necessity of being right."

I said, "Yeah, and when you have the necessity of being right, no one else can give anything to you. You have to be the only source, which means when someone gives you a great idea, you can't even receive it because you have to be right. You won't allow other people to show you a different possibility. You have to choose what you've already decided is right—and that's not the same thing as correct."

There are a lot of things that we do, and we appear to do them because we wish to be right. We try to justify the things we do by saying, "I did this because ____." No. There is no reason or justification for what you did. The *because* looks for why you did it, as though once you see why you did it, you won't do it anymore. It's simply, "I did this." You did it. You can ask, "What is this? What do I do with it? Can I change it? And if so, how do I change it?" Don't bother with, "I did it because ____." The moment you go to because you are justifying your judgments of what you chose.

In the utopian ideal, you have to strive to get it right. Have you been seeking your entire life to finally get it right? And have you ever gotten it right? I want to give you a new ideal: Seek to always be wrong. There is a lot more joy in that idea. It's easy to know when you're wrong. It's when you're doing everything you want, tasting everything you want, and doing what everybody tells you not to do. Then you're wrong and bad.

Would you consider losing the construct of being right?

Scan for more information

Happily Ever After

Are you invested in the search for the *ideal scene* in your relationship? A lot of people do this. Have you ever done the thing of looking for the perfect man or woman for you? If someone actually sees you for five seconds, you decide he or she is perfect. You say, "This is the perfect person. My ideal scene has just shown up." Then you discover it ain't necessarily so. You couldn't see what actually was because you were distracted by your concept of what was ideal. You divorced yourself and your awareness the moment you went into conclusion and said, "He's perfect. She's perfect. He's the ideal scene. She's the ideal scene. He's the one I'm looking for. She's the one I'm looking for."

I see people trying to create a construct around this all the time. They meet somebody, and as soon as they hug that person, they disappear into the illusion of the utopian ideal that this is going to turn out to be the relationship they have been looking for. They had a twenty-second hug—and a universe got constructed around it. In trying to construct the future the twenty-second hug created, they cease to be present. They're waiting for the moment in which their ideal scene is going to come to fruition.

I look at somebody and I say, "Wow! Wonderful! Okay, never mind." That's because I ask, "How will this be three months, six months and nine months down the road? How will this work out with everybody concerned?" I recently had the experience of running into a lady and thinking, "I could create a great relationship with this person." Then I asked, "Okay, so how would that work out for her?"

I said, "Well, it would work out perfectly for me." Then I said, "Wait a minute. What does she want?" Once I spotted what she wanted, I thought, "I can't fulfill what she wants. I can't be what she wants and needs in her life. I can't be what she is looking for in a relationship." So, I found somebody who would work for her and introduced them to one another.

Would you be willing to consider the possibility of losing the

construct of the ideal scene as the creation of your life?

Marriage and Happily Ever After

Happily ever after is another one of the utopian concepts. It's right up there with all the stuff about love and sex. You will know when you find the right person, your one true love, your Prince Charming, who will ride up on the white horse and sweep you away. Or maybe it's your princess, whose foot fits the glass slipper. You will ride off together into the sunset to live in your castle happily ever after.

Marriage is a utopian ideal of magnitude. The truth is that very few marriages actually work. Utopian concepts are anything but practical and workable. All of them are based on the illusion that if you give up your awareness, you can have a great relationship. Have you played that game? Was it fun for a while? Temporarily. It usually lasts about eight weeks, until you get pissed off.

My book, *Divorceless Relationship,* is about how not to divorce yourself when you're in a relationship. At the time I wrote it, I didn't realize that I was talking about conceptual constructs—but it's clear now that I was. Pretty much everybody has a utopian concept of marriage. So, you need to be aware. There are a few people who aren't dedicated to this particular conceptual construct, but they have five or six other constructs they're committed to. Those are the things that are really important to them.

If the man you're interested in has a conceptual construct of what marriage means—and he probably does—you've got to find out what that means to him. You've got to ask him questions like, "If we get married, what's that going to mean to you? What is it you want from me?" You have to see the places he is going to function from that you don't want to function from. Recognize that you will most likely have to change to fit that construct.

What does it cost you, what have you paid to have *marriage* and *happily ever after* as your reality? This is not about consequences. It's that you have to exchange something for what you get. What do you have to give up? You have to give up you. You have to give up your awareness.

You may also have to separate or divorce and give up your relationship. Divorce is okay if you don't have kids or your kids are old enough. If they're not old enough, it may not be an option. You may need to make the marriage work until the kids are old enough to comprehend what's going on.

Once you have kids, you have a whole different construct that you need to function from, because you make a commitment to them for the next eighteen to 300 years. You have to look after their needs. It's no longer just about what you want. It has to be the Kingdom of We. It's about what your child needs. If your daughter needs her mother and her father, you have to learn how to create your marriage in a way that works for you, a way that makes your husband happy but doesn't make you unhappy and that keeps your daughter content that everything will work out and life will be good. You have to show her a different possibility by being who you are regardless of the circumstances. That's a tall order, but you can do it.

Family

There is also a utopian ideal of what *family* is going to be. What payment do you have to make to keep that ideal in existence? You've been paying it for four trillion years. How long do you expect this to go on? This utopian ideal stuff is your long-term debting system. If you don't feel in debt because of your utopian ideals, I'm here to tell you that you are. What are you paying to be a parent to your child? (who may have actually been your parent) What are you not allowing in your life because you don't want to lose your family?

I have a friend who thought family was everything. She believed that everyone in a family would back each other up and take care of one another. Then her father, who was a multimillionaire, died and her half-brother took her to court and managed to get all the father's resources in his name—with nothing for my friend. At that point, she realized that the only thing that is thicker than blood is money.

Religion and Spirituality

Then there are the utopian concepts related to *religion* and *spirituality*. The utopian concept for religion is that religion is the source of all goodness. Let's say your boyfriend or your husband is dedicated to religion or spirituality. He will never look at or deal with anything that comes close to challenging that ideal. When you recognize that you are married to somebody who functions from that utopian ideal, you either have to step into his utopian concept and live from that point of view, which is where you give up you, or you have to absolutely let him have his ideal, encourage him to enjoy it and don't step into it—ever.

The idea of being selfless is based on the utopian ideal that religion and spirituality are the source for awareness. Are religion and spirituality the source for awareness? No, *you're* the source for awareness.

Religion, churches and cults are just another set of answers. Do they ask you questions to get you to see that you know? Or do they give you their answers? If they ask a question at all, it's usually, "How do you fit in this world?" not "What is your world? Where do you fit in your world? What in your world could create a better universe?"

Self and Higher Self

Self is another one of the constructs of the utopian ideal. It's the idea that there is a self that is you. Is *self* you? Is self infinite being? No, self is finite being, according to the confines of this reality.

When people say, "Your higher self would want something better," I ask, "An infinite being would have a higher self based on what?" I am in question of everything. I don't believe what anybody says. Not anybody—including me.

Higher self is the idea that there is a separation of you from you and a better version of you. What's true is that having all of you, the bad self, the good self, the crappy self, the okay self, the fat self, the ugly self, the beautiful self—all of you—the good, the bad and the ugly, is the higher self.

Instead of acknowledging this, you keep trying to determine what you shouldn't do or be in order to determine what you *should* do or be, so you can be what you've decided you aren't because you wouldn't decide you needed to be that if you were it. (If you understood that, you're doing way better than most people!) You only decide you need to be something that you've already decided you aren't.

What are you paying, what have you paid, what payment do you have to make to maintain and entrain to the conceptual constructs of the utopian reality you are trying to live by? Everything that is times a godzillion, will you destroy and uncreate it all? Right and wrong, good and bad, POC and POD, all 9, shorts, boys and beyonds.

What are you refusing to lose, that if you would lose it,

would give you all of you?

Money and the Creation of Money

Most everyone has ideas about how money should be, and they keep trying to buy into conceptual constructs of *how money is created*. By and large, they believe money is created by work. But that's not it. Money is created by request—not by work. You don't have to work harder in order to create more money; you simply have to request more money in order to have more money.

Recently I was looking at the money I was supposed to be making in Access Consciousness®, and I wanted to find out how much I was paying the people who work for me. I got everybody to fess up to how much money they were earning. It was interesting, because most of them had tried desperately not to have any awareness of the amount they were making. They were trying to keep it secret from themselves. Several people had their income increase by as much as twenty percent right after they admitted how much they made. It was something they hadn't been willing to look at.

I am upfront. I say, "This is the money I make. This is how it works for me. This is what I have to do." When I got clear about how much money I was spending on all the people who work for me, I said, "That's not enough. I need more money and they need more money." Then all of a sudden, we started making more money.

If you are avoiding doing accounting or looking at your money situation, you are trying to avoid creation. It's a way you limit the amount of money you can make. Creation can only occur if you know how much money you need, how much you would like to have, how much you can have and how much more would work better for you. Presently you are not asking for what you'd like. You are trying to function within a structure in which you don't have to know, so as long as you have more at the end of the month than you did at the beginning, you're okay. That's trying to create from the idea that money is created from illusion, not from awareness.

I knew a lady who inherited some money. She had a trust fund. But in the twenty years that somebody else had been handling the trust fund, it had not increased in value at all. That was twenty years of the greatest growth in the market the United States had ever seen. That portfolio should have doubled, but it hadn't. Her advisors were mismanaging it. You have to look at how you are creating money rather than expecting somebody else to be in control of how you create it. The lady is now actually paying attention to her money and she has turned everything around. The more you start being you and the more you start taking care of you, the more your money will increase.

Don't avoid awareness of your finances; get clear about them. When you do, you can create more to a degree that will surprise you because you will be asking from a different place. If you are not willing to be clear about your money, then there is a level of change that you cannot institute in people.

You could also try asking the question, "How can I earn ten times this amount of money doing something different and not working so hard?" Money is created by request. You have to ask.

Contribution Is About Energy

A friend of mine who makes plenty of money is having a relationship with a man who makes very little. She really likes this man, but it was a problem for her that he wasn't paying his "fair share."

I said to her, "You got involved with somebody who has no money and now you are trying to drive him to make more money. Where is your energy going for the creation of money? Is it going into him? Or is it going into you? You are using more energy to get him to make money so he can pay his share than you are using to create money for you."

"You have the conceptual construct that everybody should earn equal amounts of money and pay their fair share, and you are beating him to death to get him to go out and earn his own money. How is that working for you? It doesn't work because you are trying to force him to do something he doesn't really want to do. He wants to be a kept man."

By keeping her conceptual construct in place, she was destroying her relationship, which was actually a good one that worked for her.

> What are you paying, what have you paid, what is the payment you have to give to keep your conceptual constructs of your utopian reality? Everything that is times a godzillion, will you destroy and uncreate it all? Right and wrong, good and bad, POC and POD, all 9, shorts, boys and beyonds.

Everything Contributes to Us

What my friend wasn't looking at is that people contribute to us. And things contribute to us. Their contribution is about energy. Some people are a contribution to our life, yet they don't produce a direct result of money. But because of the contribution they are making to us, money starts to flow in our life. For me, this happens with horses. I spend a lot of money taking care of my horses. They don't directly bring in any money, yet as a result of their contribution to me, more money comes to me—because contribution is about energy. My daughter's baby is a huge contribution to her life. She could say, "Look at all the money I have to spend for this kid." Or she could take a different point of view and ask, "Has money become more difficult or easier since I had the kid?" That's the question to ask.

My friend could ask, "Has money been easier since I got the guy—or harder?" She's trying to make life difficult for him so he pays his fair share; she doesn't realize he is contributing so much energy to her that she is making more money. Contribution is about energy. You have to be willing to see what contributes to you without having a point of view about it.

Expand Your Life and Your Finances Expand

Finances are not the sum total of the expansion of your life. You want to get to the point where you create your choices, not based on your economic conditions or what you wish to create economically, but on the basis of, "How is this going to create a future in which everything improves?" People have become so fixated on their economic utopian ideals that they forget about creating a scenario in which their entire future expands—including their finances. They don't seem to realize that when they expand their life, their finances will expand as well. I often see people who come to Access Consciousness® classes because they want a more expanded life. Then, "by accident," their finances improve.

"If I Choose This, What Will This Create?"

When people say things like, "This action or activity creates money, and that other thing doesn't create money," they're speaking from the utopian constructs of this reality. "This is going to make me money" is a conclusion—not a question. You think that if you come to conclusion, you will create the money or the future you desire, but it doesn't work that way. You have to be willing to function from the *awareness* of what will create the future you would like to have—not from the conclusion of what you've decided you want the future to be.

In the past, whenever I considered doing something, I would ask, "Will this expand my agenda? Will this make me money?" If I got a yes, I'd say, "Okay, I'll do it." Did I know how it was going to expand my agenda? No. Did I see a direct result between what I did and the money that came in? No. Was my income going up? Yes. If my income was going up with all the things I was doing, I'd continue to do them. I don't cut things out based on not seeing the direct way in which something has brought me money. Even with my horses, I don't do that.

However, I recently realized we had to change that question—because every man has a penis named Agenda. Whenever it comes to a woman, the answer to the question, "Will this expand my agenda?" is always yes. So, we changed the question to, "If I choose this, what will this create in five years? If I don't choose this, what will this create in five years?" When you function from that, you cannot create the construct of time for a five-year period. You can have an *awareness* of a five-year period, but you can't have a *construct* of what that looks like. And what you want is the awareness of what will create the future you would like to have.

"Will You Make Me Money?"

It's not just people and animals that are a contributuion to you. The things in your life will contribute to you as well—if you ask them to. You may feel like you're the slave of the things you own. And actually, you are. You have to pay for them, you have to keep them clean, and you have to work to maintain them. You might feel like you are their servant or their minion, but you can ask them to work for you. That's what I suggest.

Before you buy anything, ask it, "If I buy you, will you make me money? If I show you off in my house, will you make me money? Will you contribute to me? Will you make my life better? Will you expand my life? Will you expand my future?" Ask these questions before you buy a car or a house, a dress or pair of shoes. With my horses, I ask, "If I buy you, will you make me money?" When it's yes, I start making more money. Do I know how it's working? No. Do I know that it's working? Yes. I am willing to know whether it's working. Most people are not.

Ask everything, including your children, if they will make you money. They can say no, but if you don't give them a job, they won't know what to do. People never ask their kids to contribute to them. They just ask their kids to be good. But what kid knows what being good means? The only way you know you're being good is if you're resisting everything you like to do. What a pathetic life that is. So, give your kids a job and show them how to contribute to you.

Teaching Kids About Money

People sometimes ask, "What do I do with my kids? They're spending all my money."

I say, "Let them spend it. How else are they going to learn what happens when they have no money?" Tell them, "This is the amount of money you have. When that's gone, you're going to have to wait until you do something." Then make them do something to get the money.

I taught my youngest son to clean ashtrays at his godfather's house so he could get an ice cream cone. There were always plenty of full ashtrays, and he made money each time he cleaned one. He was two when he was earning his ice cream money. Now, as an adult, he is fine with doing difficult jobs.

My parents didn't teach me about money. I got an allowance for smiling and being good, and when people didn't give me money for smiling and being good, I'd ask, "What did I do wrong?" Giving your kids an allowance is fine. But I love it when I see kids doing things to make money.

Teach your kids about money. Let them have money. Let them spend their money on whatever they wish to spend it on—and ask them to put away ten percent of anything they earn so that they always have money for a future.

They will learn that when they spend money on something that breaks instantly or doesn't work for them that they made a "bad" choice. You've got to let them make bad choices so they learn what a good choice is for them. Choice creates awareness. So, if they choose to spend their money on something that doesn't work, they will learn. And teach them how to have fun with money. I used to ask my kids, "Who could you give money to that it would change their reality? If you gave that money to somebody, would it change their reality?"

When I was a kid, I would spend my allowance on my friends. I thought it was really fun to buy pie for them, rather than my having pie by myself and their having nothing. Their families didn't have money. My family didn't either, but they wanted me to grow up to believe I might have money if I worked hard enough. My point of view was, "I'm going to have money, and that's all there is to it. I see the way rich people live and I see the way we live. I'm not living like we live."

My sister has chosen to be like my mother when it comes to money, so I have a lot more fun with money than she does. She can hold onto a penny so tight it screams. She doesn't spend anything that she can avoid spending. I spend when it works to create a different reality for me and everybody else.

You've got to recognize that if you create money today, your future will be different tomorrow. You create money today, so that you can have a future that has a different reality.

A Different Universe Is Available to You

Please look at these constructs and utopian ideals. A different universe is available to you if you're willing to have it. You've got to get that choosing a limitation is a choice—not a necessity. You've spent your whole life choosing from the supposed necessity of what is right to choose. That's not a choice; it's actually a no-choice universe. You've got to get over the idea of necessity and rightness.

Do you get that you've been in an idealistic search mode? How many conceptual constructs are you using to create your personal idealistic search mode? Everything that is time a godzillion, will you destroy and uncreate it all? Right and wrong, good and bad, POC and POD, all 9, shorts, boys and beyonds.

You are the carrier of the virus of consciousness. You'll go out and infect the entire world with it if you're not careful. We have started to create a permeation of consciousness in the world. I ask you to start functioning from greater awareness. This is what you're here to do—to have that awareness and be that awareness and to create a change that's possible beyond this reality. If that's what you want to do, come play.

What have you decided you can't let go of that's creating

limitation in your life?

◊

THE WILLINGNESS TO LOSE EVERYTHING

Not only do you have to be willing to lose

your constructs and utopian ideals;

you also have to be willing to lose your convictions

and points of view.

Once you're willing to lose everything,

a different possibility can show up for you.

You will be unfettered by limitation.

Commitment and the Willingness to Lose Everything

The utopian point of view is that commitment requires total devotion and delivery. You think commitment means you are required to deliver what you promised. This goes along with the idea that commitment is slavery. But commitment is not slavery. I'm not talking about an ideal scene in which somebody makes a commitment and becomes a slave forever. True commitment is the recognition of what you would like most to be committed to. My commitment is to total consciousness no matter what it looks like, no matter what it takes. I am married to that idea. Does that commitment to consciousness include a relationship? No. Does that exclude a relationship? No. Does it include having lots of money? No. Does it exclude having lots of money? No. It opens the door to all possibilities.

And here's the thing: You can be committed to something and still be willing to lose the thing you're committed to. For instance, I am totally committed to Access Consciousness® and I would lose it all in a heartbeat.

Making a Total Commitment to You

You may think that losing something means giving it up or that you can't have it—but losing something means you get more of it. For example, when you make a commitment to you, you have to be willing to lose you in order to have more of you. You are aware of who you are and you have no point of view about it. You know you can change if you choose. That's the most important thing to get. You know you can change if you choose. If you don't have that, then you haven't created a place where you are in a constant state of creation. You are trying to function from the constructs and limitations of the past.

That place of constructs and limitations is where you're functioning from right now. You have decided who you are—and you don't realize that decision is crippling you. You think your point of view of you is you. It is not. A point of view is not you. Every point of view you have about you creates the not you that's messing you up, so you don't have to be committed to you.

Are you willing to lose all the things about you that aren't really you? What about your looks? You created your looks. Your looks are a great weapon or a great tool. You may not be willing to lose them. If you're not willing to lose them, you create a constant state of judging your looks and in so doing, you create what you judge to be the wrongness of the way you look. You have to be willing to lose your heritage, your nationality, your race, your sexual orientation and anything else you think identifies and defines who you are, because whenever you attempt to define anything, you contract your awareness. Whatever you think you are, you are not. Why is that? Because you, as you, are not definable.

Are You Willing to Risk Losing Everything?

People don't want to know they can lose anything. They think losing is the worst thing they can do. But if you're willing to risk losing everything, you open the door to all that is possible. Four times in my life, I have lost everything I owned. I started over again. For me, the idea of losing everything is, "So what? Is it going to kill me? No. Is it going to change things? Yes." That's all it's going to do; it's going to change things.

You need to recognize that energy never ceases to exist, so you can't really lose anything, anyway, because energy always is. Energy can change, it can alter, it can take different forms, but it cannot be destroyed. Therefore, the idea of loss is the greatest lie we buy.

I see thousands of people trying to hold on to what they've got. They're saying, "Dear God, please don't let me lose everything because if I lose everything I have, I will have nothing." No. You have everything when you have you. But you don't consider it valuable to have you. You think that the things you have—your money, your house, your car or your clothes—are more valuable to you than you.

Years ago after Hurricane Andrew occurred in Florida, I saw a man on the news. He was standing in front of the bare slab where his house used to be. He said, "Well, I moved down here from Indiana to retire, and I brought all my worldly goods with me. And now all I have is a slab. But I still have me." After the Northridge earthquake in California, a couple were on the news. The man said, "My wife and I were naked in our bed in our third-floor condo. We felt everything starting to rock and roll, and the next thing we knew, we were down on the ground floor, and there was nothing around but a pair of shorts for me and for my wife, a robe. The only thing we have left is our wedding picture, but we still have each other."

The reality is—when you lose everything and you still have you, you have everything worth having.

What's the most important thing in your life? What has the highest value for you? That's your hierarchy of value. Maybe you've decided, "The most valuable thing in my life is my hair." That's the one thing you're not willing to lose. Then suddenly, something occurs—like cancer and chemo—and the thing you were unwilling to lose, you have now lost. This happened to a friend of mine. She used to have massive amounts of beautiful hair. Her hair was her pride and joy. It was at the top of her hierarchy of value—and then she lost it all. This is the kind of thing we do to ourselves to make us seek a larger universe, and in my friend's case, it worked. After she lost her hair, all kinds of amazing possibilities suddenly opened up for her. If she hadn't lost her hair, she wouldn't have chosen different. And that's the one thing you have to be willing to do—to choose different.

The willingness to lose everything is the place where you begin to have true choice. If you're not willing to lose everything, you make your choices based on what you're not willing to lose. I have a friend who was not willing to lose his daughter. The daughter got involved with a ratbag of a guy my friend didn't like, a guy he actually wanted to kill because he treated her so badly. My friend tried to go to bat for his daughter, and she said, "Dad, I'm a grown woman. Leave me alone."

My friend knew he had to be willing to lose his daughter to this ratbag—but he wasn't willing to do that, so we did a little process, and he got over it. He saw that he had created his whole life based on the idea that he wasn't willing to lose her. He said, "Okay, she has just given me my walking papers. She no longer needs me. I am willing to lose her." He recognized that having her need him had been one of his criteria for a successful life. After he became willing to give her up and let her go to the guy, she found out on her own that he was a ratbag and she left him.

The truth is—you can gain everything by what you're willing to lose. You don't have the capacity to truly choose everything until you're willing to lose anything and everything.

Once you have that, you see that whatever it is you were holding on to is not a necessity. You've got to be willing to lose your kids. You've got to be willing to lose your family. You've got to be willing to lose everything. When you're willing to lose it all, when you have nothing that you have to hold onto, true choice begins.

You don't realize a different possibility can exist when you're willing to lose the thing you think you can't lose. And the beauty of it is that when you're willing to lose it, you can have it. You can't truly have anything until you're willing to let it go.

Who or what are you owned by, that if you were not owned by them or it, would allow you to commit to you? Everything that is times a godzillion, will you destroy and uncreate it all? Right and wrong, good and bad, POC and POD, all 9, shorts, boys and beyonds.

What if you lost everything, and as a result,

you had the capacity to choose anything?

Scan for more information

Losing Your Convictions and Fixed Points of View

Whenever you have a conviction or a fixed point of view about anything, you have come to conclusions, decisions, judgments, and computations in order to create it.

A *conviction* is a strong belief that excludes doubt. That's pretty interesting, because when you have a conviction, you've been convicted; you're in the jail of your own point of view. You have judged, juried and placed yourself in the slammer of your own limitations. Conviction puts you in a place where you are in reaction. People who are convinced about something, of necessity, always have to see the rightness of their conviction. They're in the temple of righteousness. Their intention is to cut your heart out with their conviction. They are right in their point of view that you're wrong, regardless of what viewpoint you take.

A *point of view* is a position from which something is observed; it's a particular way of looking at something, which means you can only occupy one place in the universe at any one time. When you take a point of view, you eliminate space and compress it down to one point. This is where you create a limitation because you cannot be aware of any other choice, possibility or contribution. And you can't be in multiple places. A point of view is different from awareness. *Awareness* is seeing what you can see—and not having a point of view about it; otherwise, you may be trying to create something that does not exist.

You choose to take fixed points of view, thinking that if you take enough of them, you'll finally be solid and real. I'm not quite sure why you would like to be solid and real. A turd is solid and real too, and it smells. And so do some of your fixed points of view. You take on fixed points of view about what you're supposed to be, what you're supposed to do, how something is supposed to be, or what's supposed to happen. None of these give you the freedom to choose.

We create ourselves as individuals by our fixed points of view. It's the way we maintain our separation from ourselves as well as everyone and everything else. We become energetically limited by our fixed points of view. Years ago, I was doing a class in Texas. I was working with a Mexican lady, and I asked her to destroy and uncreate some points of view she brought up that were limiting her. She said, "You don't understand. You *weddos* don't understand what it's like to have people be prejudiced against you."

The word *weddo* is Mexican slang for someone who has a pale complexion or light hair. It is often used in a derogatory way, like "whitey," and she was using it in that way. I gave what she said back to her a hundredfold. I said, "You female chauvinist pig. You have just defined racism to the nth degree. I am not a *weddo*. I am not a white person. I am an infinite being. Thank you for your judgment."

Everyone in the room was sitting with their mouth open, waiting to see what was going to happen next. They couldn't believe I would say such a thing.

I was taking no prisoners. I was saying, "Don't tell me I'm a white guy who judges people. I am not. I am an infinite being and I will allow you to choose to be that as well. If you want to be a prejudiced bitch, I will let you be a prejudiced bitch. If you want to be an infinite being, that's a different story. Let's play. There is possibility in the world—or there is limitation."

It was, "Now, would you like to give up your prejudiced points of view? Or would you like to continue to berate me and try to make me small? Because that's what you're trying to do with your prejudice."

She said, "I'll give them up," and everything she was holding onto broke apart.

You buy points of view in an attempt to define you. You use a fixed point of view to define—and definition, by definition alone, is limitation. If I say, "You're an Indian," does that define things for you?

Does that define things for other people? Why do people want to define things? They want to define things so they can choose what to reject. The purpose of definition is to choose what you reject.

How many fixed points of view are you refusing to lose because

you think that if you lose them, you'll lose you?

If you have no point of view, then you can take any point of view. You can choose the point of view you wish to use. Then, if you wish, you can choose another—or have none at all.

You may think you don't exist unless you have a point of view. Most people do. You have lots of nice fixed points of view in order to maintain your connection to the past, so you can identify who you are based on who you were, so you can be who you will never be again, because that's the way to get to be the future that you're never willing to have.

How many fixed points of view do you have that are creating your limitations and your prejudiced points of view about you? Do you get that you are prejudiced against you? That's unbelievable. To judge you—what a travesty. What an unkindness. What a brutality. You are an amazing miracle that you don't see. You don't get the miracle that you are and you don't incorporate it into your reality. You keep pretending that somehow it can't be true. Why is the miracle of you the only thing in life that can't be true? You judge you and create separation from you and everybody around you by your fixed points of view. Is that a good idea, a bad idea or just not the best choice?

Changing your reality is really fun. It's better than changing your clothes. You may not want to know that. Your underwear, you will change. Your reality, you won't change. But your reality stinks more than your underwear.

What fixed points of view do you have that you have defined as you? Everything that is times a godzillion, will you destroy and uncreate it all? Right and wrong, good and bad, POC and POD, all 9, shorts, boys and beyonds.What fixed point of view do you have that you absolutely will not lose that keep you from having all of you? Everything that is times a godzillion, will you destroy and uncreate it all? Right and wrong, good and bad, POC and POD, all 9, shorts, boys and beyonds.

How many fixed points of view do you have

that create the lie of what you're not willing to be?

You're Way Better Than You Think You Are

Many people have adopted points of view about what they're not good at. They say, "I'm not good at math," "I'm not good at fixing things," or "I'm not good with my hands." You would decide you're not good at something for what reason? To make sure you can get someone else to do those things. It's called control. I always say I'm not good at computers. But if nobody's around and I want to get something accomplished on the computer, I manage to get it done. Meanwhile, back at the ranch, I get people to do things for me because I'm so bad at computers. Does that work for me? Yes. I'm willing to look at it and see it for what it is. I'm a manipulating son-of-a-gun who will get people to do things for me that I don't want to do. That's wrong based on what? Nothing, as far as I'm concerned.

This is different from creating a fixed point of view that you're not good at something so you can make it real that you're not good at it—so when you manipulate somebody into doing it for you, you actually don't know how to do it.

Or maybe you do some version of, "I don't know how to do that. I'm a girl. Can you help me, please?" Or maybe you do, "Bug off! I can do it all myself. I don't need any of you men." Are those all fixed points of view? Yes, they are.

I worked with a woman whose whole life was about the way her father had stopped her from doing things. It was the lie she was using to create the limitations of her life. Once she recognized it, she said, "Well, that's silly. Why would I choose that? I don't need to choose that." She lost that point of view and got to the place where she is now able to choose something different.

Everybody in this reality tries to tell you what your problem is. They say things like, "Your problem is you have a broken heart," "Your problem is your parents screwed you up," "Your problem is you don't have enough money," "Your problem is the men in your life were abusive, "Your problem is…." Those things are points of view. And they're lies. Until somebody is willing to show you what you're choosing and where you're choosing from, it's hard to choose something different.

I never try to tell you what your problem is. What am I trying to tell you? I'm trying to tell you that you're way better than you think you are. You resist that and you create confusion for what reason? What are you trying to maintain by not having clarity? A façade of you being less than what you actually are. You create that façade for whom? Everybody else. Then you buy it as true. That's not a good purchase. Take that back for a full refund.

What fixed points of view do you have

that allow you to make sure you don't ever have to be you?

Losing Your Fallback Position

If you're going to make a commitment to you, there's something else you have to lose. You have to lose your fallback position. A fallback position is a contingency plan for your worst-case scenario. It is the solution to the utopian ideal you have bought when it doesn't work. It's the strategy you take when your primary position is threatened. It is a way to protect and vindicate yourself. Your fallback position is your insurance policy.

It's also called leaving through the back door. It's taking off quietly without making a fuss rather than facing up to the challenge. It's a way you pretend you don't have any power. No one has had your back in the past, and you have never had your back, either. So, your idea of having your back has been to escape. That was the quickest, easiest, fastest and safest way you could come up with to protect yourself. Most back doors are about how to change something without actually changing anything. That's the reason you have a back door—so you can change without changing.

Having a back door is about opening the front door so the thing that will give you everything you want in your life can show up. You open the front door, and at the same time, you've got a wedge holding the back door open so you can escape before you actually have to achieve that change. You're looking for a way to get out more than you're looking for a way to get in.

If you have a sense of urgency about change, it's probably an activation of your back door. You build your image on top of your back door so that nobody will see what your back door is, and you can continue to use it. Your back door is, "Nobody will ever see the true me, including me." How is that working for you? It's not!

Most of us have a place in us where we think that if somebody is asking us to be who we truly are, they're going to use it as a source of abuse. When you were a kid, the few times you showed up as you, somebody abused you for that. You learned to create a back door so that you would never make that mistake again.

What mistake are you not willing to make, that if you would make it, would give you all of you? Everything that is times a godzillion, will you destroy and uncreate it all? Right and wrong, good and bad, POC and POD, all 9, shorts, boys and beyonds.

Total commitment to you is the willingness to lose everything—including your back door. I wish to have total consciousness, which means I am willing to lose everything that isn't conscious, everything I'm not conscious of, everything that would lead to unconsciousness, and everyone who believes unconsciousness is more valuable than consciousness.

Death As a Back Door

Many of us have death as a back door. We think, "Well, if it gets really bad, I can always die." I know that place well. On the last day of a class we did in Australia a few years ago, I got really ill and ended up in the hospital. When that occurred, I realized that the one thing I wasn't willing to lose was death as my final option. My point of view was that death created the winning hand for me; it was my ace card. It would allow me to leave when I chose. It was my way out of everything I didn't like. Death was my back door.

You may have death as a back door as well. Somewhere in your universe, you may have the point of view, "Well, if push comes to shove, I can always die." It's a safe way out. Or maybe you think, "I want to die while I'm still young and beautiful so it's a tragedy when I go. People will mourn my death; such a tragic loss—so young and beautiful."

As long as you're not willing to lose death, you will never be committed to living to the fullest you can live. The unwillingness to lose death keeps you from having total consciousness. When you are finally willing to lose death, you have to be totally conscious in every moment of every day about every choice you make, because death is not the final option. You no longer have death as the final future. You now have to choose to live.

What choices would you have to make if death wasn't

your primary option?

Are you willing to lose the things in your life that don't work for you? Yes. But you're not willing to lose what you've decided, concluded, judged and computed is valuable to you. Your hierarchy of value is, "I will lose what I don't like, but I have to keep what I do like." You don't ask, "Is this thing I value a limitation in any way, shape or form?"

Whatever you've decided you have to hold onto becomes the least of what you're capable of—not the most.

Leaving on a Dime

You may be one of those people—and there are many of them—who want to able to leave on a dime. The one thing you're not willing to lose is the ability to get out of town fast, whether it's getting away from your relationship, your job or some other situation. Leaving on a dime is your "get out of jail free" card. It is your fallback position; it's what you do when something isn't working. Being able to leave on a dime is your solution to never being committed. You say, "How do I get out of this? I can leave anybody on a dime."

When a friend of mine and her partner were buying a house together, she froze and wanted to throw up because that was way too much of a commitment. I told her, "Well, you can always leave on a dime and lose all the money you invested."

She said, "Oh! Okay, fine," and she was over it. She just needed to know that she had a back door. That's the thing of recognizing the place somebody is functioning from and realizing what they have to have as their weasel clause—their back door—and giving it to them.

You've determined and decided too many times that leaving is the way to have you. Yes, leaving can be a way to get you back when you've given yourself up to create a relationship. This has been successful for you in the past. That is why you keep choosing the back door rather than something more expansive. When you do, "I can leave on a dime," you're doing the same thing you've always done, and it creates the same result it did the last time you left.

When you've got your eye on the back door, you don't have to make a commitment. If you're maintaining your back door so you can get the hell out, it means you will not commit to anyone, and most impressively, not to you. You can't totally create your life, your relationship or anything else because you are always looking for a way out. You are not willing to be infinite. You'd rather be able to leave on a dime than have infinite choice, infinite possibilities, infinite question, infinite creation and infinite capacity for anything.

Losing vs Leaving

Have you misapplied and misidentified *leaving* as *losing*? *Lose* means not have anymore. Leave means go away. Maybe you look around and you think everybody is going to leave you. That's because you've already committed to leaving them. You think, "I've got to see when they're going to leave me, so I can leave them first because I don't want to be the one who has been left." You can leave anyone at the drop of a hat. On a dime, at the drop of a hat, any way you look at it, it's about getting out first.

You don't have to think about leaving when you are willing to lose other people. When you're willing to lose them, they can constantly change. You are willing to lose who they are today, which means you are constantly capable of change and so are they. You are willing to lose them—but not leave them—so you don't have to hold onto them. You are also willing to lose what you've decided is you. You don't need that idea in order to know who are.

I am committed to consciousness. Can I lose anyone? Yes. Will I leave anyone? No. Leaving is like saying, "If you won't play by my rules, I'm taking my marbles and going home." If you're scared to lose your partner, you have to limit the amount of change you can have. You have to limit the amount of change he or she can have. Is that working for you? Leaving is easier than being committed to change. Most people are willing to leave their lives on a dime, rather than change so they become more.

The Kingdom of We

When you choose to get married, your commitment is not to marriage. In a marriage, you should be committed to you and the other person. That's the Kingdom of We. The two of you are doing something together; therefore, you should be committed to that person. And he or she should be committed to you. I don't care who you marry, whether it's a male or female or whether you have legal documents; if you are committed to one another, it's still a marriage. When you choose from the Kingdom of We, it's not about choosing for you and against the other person. Nor do you choose for you and exclude the other person. You choose for you *and* everybody else; you choose what will expand all possibilities, including your own. When you do this, people around you realize their choice will expand by your choice, and they will contribute to your choices, not resist them.

I am not going to try to convince you that you should commit to you and the other person in your life. I know I can't convince you of anything. You've got to see whether the way you're operating is working for you. If you don't realize that it isn't working, you will always have a back door. It's your escape route; it's the way you get out of being committed. You have multiple fallback positions, so if one doesn't work out, you can choose another. You think it's best to have at least half a dozen of them, so you know you have a way out, no matter what happens. You have decided that having a back door is the perfect choice for you.

You would lose your back door if you actually made a commitment to anyone or anything (including you or your life) because your back door keeps you from having to make a commitment for any length of time if you can avoid it. It's not necessary to know what your back doors are. It's just necessary to know that you have a back door that you're not willing to lose. And if you're not willing to lose your back door, you will always have to stand with your hand on the doorknob so you can get out fast.

The Kingdom of True Choice

So, it's not about having a fallback position, an escape hatch or a back door. It's not about dying, leaving on a dime, going to live in another country or any of the multitude of exit plans you may have. It's about having the Kingdom of True Choice, which is the willingness to lose all the back doors you are holding onto. In the Kingdom of True Choice, there is an unlimited menu of things to choose from; however, when you are unwilling to let go of your back door position, you go into an either/or universe, where you're choosing for you or against you. You say, "I can stay or I can go. Those are my two choices."

You keep thinking that if you make a choice, you won't have any other choices, which means you will not allow yourself to have the total abundance and the total possibilities that are available to you. You choose a life that is small to make sure that your choices give you what you've determined, decided, judged and computed you deserve to have. You will never receive anything that you've decided is undeserved. Receiving a gift has got to be really tough for you.

Choosing to Be You

You may feel that if you don't choose the back door that is "yours," you are losing your right and your capacity to be you. It's easy to be you when nobody else is around, but it's hard to be you in the midst of others, because you've never chosen for you. Choosing to be you, regardless of whether anybody else is around, is a whole different universe. That's the Kingdom of True Choice. You have to be willing to be you, regardless of what's going on in the rest of the world. I am willing to be me whether anybody likes it or not, whether anybody receives it or not, no matter what occurs.

Is your life enough? No? Then ask for more. Demand of yourself: "I don't care what I lose. I am going to have a life that's more than this." You have a level of intelligence, a level of capacity and a level of generosity that few people on the planet have. Are you using it?

No. Why not? Because you're trying to make sure you can leave on a dime. You're trying to make sure you don't have so much money that people want to take it from you. You are trying to be less than you are.

There's no need to figure out what your back door is. All you have to do is ask, "What am I doing, limiting myself here? I would not choose something greater than this for what reason?"

What are you refusing to lose, that if you lost it,

would give you a level of awareness

that would go beyond the utopian constructs of reality?

Consciousness Is Only a Choice Away

Gandhi said, "Be the change you'd like to see in the world." Why is *not* using your level of capacity, intelligence and generosity more important to you than being more of what you are and creating the change in the world that you would like to see?

Each of us can be the element of change we have been unwilling to be. Until now, you have only been willing to be the ideal, which creates others having conflict with you, judging you, not seeing you and not wanting to be around you—but none of those are what you are looking for. You don't ask, "What else can I generate and create that's beyond anything I ever knew was possible?"

You think that to be different requires separation from the oneness you are. This is not so. To be truly different requires oneness. The most different person in the world is the person who functions from oneness and consciousness. If you're truly willing to function from oneness, everything and everyone changes around you.

Do you really want a difference? Try being conscious.

If you have consciousness, you will enjoy everything in life. For me, consciousness has a sense of peace with it. It's an open-ended universe in which anything becomes possible, everything is available, and the choices you make determine how you're willing to be with yourself and everybody around you. Peace and joy go hand in hand. You have a sense of peace and joy, and a sense of possibility, expansion and gratitude for everything and everyone around you.

Most people are not willing to have peace and joy. They are willing to have fun to a certain extent, but what they've defined as fun is something that seems manically happy. They put on a fake face so they can prove they're happy when they're not. I'm not talking about pretending to be happy. I'm talking about opening the door to a possibility of happiness that you probably haven't considered.

Sometimes people temporarily access real peace and joy as a possibility, but they seldom maintain that possibility. There are many things on this planet that will give you the illusion for a short time that you're getting there. Metaphysics does it; churches, cults and religions do it. I did all kinds of metaphysical practices and I'd feel really good for five or ten days, then all of a sudden, I'd be back in my shit again. I don't desire for people to be back in their shit. I desire for them never to be able to go back to their shit. That's what I'm shooting for with all of this.

I am looking for a different result than most people are looking for. I am interested in how we take the awareness that is you and expand it so your life expands. Consciousness is the way to do that. When you start choosing consciousness, all of a sudden, doors open.

Do you have the fixed point of view that you will work up to this consciousness thing? Do you think, "I will choose consciousness a little bit at a time? Eventually, you might talk me into going there. But I'm not going to do that until you talk me into it totally. You'd better be a good convincer, because I doubt that anybody is going to tell me the truth."

If consciousness is years away, then you can maintain what? Your fixed points of view. If this describes you, I'm going to tell you something you're not going to like: Consciousness is not a muscle you have to build. Consciousness is only a choice away. It's a choice you have to make.

What would happen if you stepped into the space

of all that choice?

Perfect Awareness

With consciousness you will have perfect awareness. You will be aware of everything. Perfect awareness doesn't mean that everything becomes perfect. Perfect awareness means you get to be aware of everything in totality. And that's perfect.

Total awareness does not give you a comfortable reality. It just gives you a lot of awareness. Sometimes you have to be with things that are uncomfortable. They're uncomfortable because you don't want to have that degree of awareness. For example, if you had a high degree of awareness, you would have to give up making mistakes. You couldn't say, "I didn't realize what I was doing. I had no idea it was going to turn out like this." Those are the places where you are choosing to be unconscious or anti-conscious. You may think if you have less awareness it's going to be better. You don't yet realize that more awareness is going to be greater.

What are you refusing to lose, that if you would lose it, would give you total awareness of everything you could be, do, have, create and generate in life? Everything that is times a godzillion, will you destroy and uncreate it all? Right and wrong, good and bad, POC and POD, all 9, shorts, boys and beyonds.

◊

QUESTION AND TRUE CHOICE

You've been taught to ask a question in order to get the answer.

But that's not it.

The purpose of a question is to expand awareness—

not to get an answer.

Anything that does not give you a total sense of choice and possibility

is a utopian construct you've integrated into your reality.

Being the Question

We've all been taught to ask a question in order to get an answer. We've never been told that an answer stops the motion in our life that would lead us to what we desire. In Access Consciousness®, we start out by getting people to ask a question—because most people have never asked a question before. They have always looked for an answer.

The purpose of a question is to expand awareness—not to get an answer. It's a huge step toward becoming aware of possibilities. You don't want to have an answer. You want to be the question. When you are being the question, you are in a state of curiosity. You're asking, "What else is possible?" You are curious about everything in the world, including yourself. Curiosity is contagious. Curiosity is expansive. Curiosity will lead you to what you're looking for. You have no conclusions of any kind. You don't accept answers or solutions nor do you try to give solutions to other people.

As long as you're being the question, you will find your path to what you seek. Question is imperative. You have to constantly question in order to be in a state of motion. You have to be willing to be the question to find what works for you. Question maintains the place of expansion and the sense of curiosity. Curiosity has no completion—but answer does. You don't want to try to get the "right" answer, wait for an answer or decide on the answer. You want to be the question.

This is the reason I don't tell people what to do. I tell them what I've got and how I've done things. I invite them to use the tools—but I don't give them answers. Even so, people keep trying to find the ideal, and they keep trying to turn Access Consciousness® into a utopian cult. In a utopia, there is a right answer. You're never asked to question anything. You're never asked to be aware of what you're aware of. That's why we try to get people moving towards being the question.

Expansive Questions vs Contractive Questions

Recently a friend of mine wanted to change a situation in her life, and she was asking, "What question do I need to ask? What question do I need to ask?" She wasn't getting anywhere. Why was that? Because she had contracted her awareness in order to ask that question. Unfortunately, this occurs more than you might recognize.

Sometimes people think, "Well, if I ask a question about this issue, I will get clarity about it." They are looking for clarity, which means they've already decided what it is they're looking for. That's contractive. And when they don't get the answer they want, they think they didn't ask the right question. This approach has nothing to do with asking real questions or being curious about the world.

People also use the idea of being the question to create doubt, not possibility. They say things like, "I've got to question whether I chose the right answer." That's not about being aware of what is possible. And it is contractive. It's choosing doubt.

When you attempt to *be in the question* or to *create a question*, you have to contract your awareness. This was a new awareness for me. You don't want to *have a question, go into the question, be in the question, create a question* or *come to question*. All of those, to one degree or another, are a contraction of awareness. They're about making the question the answer—instead of making the question the awareness.

Another thing people do is ask "questions" that are actually conclusions with a question mark at the end: "Where is the snake that's going to bite me?" "Where is the person who's going to have sex with me?" What do those questions have to do with awareness or possibility? Nothing! These people don't ask, "What is actually possible here that I haven't considered?" That's a real question.

Or they ask so-called questions like, "How can I be more creative?" which is simply an assumption or a conclusion that they're not being as creative as they could be. A real question would be, "What additional creativity do I have available that I haven't even tapped into?" That's what you've got to look at.

When I facilitate people, I ask, "How can I educate them to see what they are capable of? How can I process them so they have access to it? What is it that I'm not contributing, that if I could or would contribute, would change their reality?"

It's not, "How do I get them to be, know, perceive or receive more?" It's, "What can I change?"

When you function from questions like:

- What is this?

- What do I do with it?

- Can I change it?

- And if so, how do I change it?

you're not trying to come to conclusion about what the question is. You're asking open questions. For example, when something is going on in my body, I ask, "What is this? What do I do with it? Can I change it? If so, how do I change it? What do I need to be or do different?"

When you ask a question, the universe has to rearrange itself. If you keep saying, "I have lived with a disability for twenty-five years," the universe assumes you want to continue to live with it. But if you ask a question like, "Body, what do you know that I don't that would change all this?" something different can show up, and when it does, you'll know, "Oh, that's what I've been asking for." You'll get it instantaneously.

The Purpose of Question Is Awareness

Most of us keep looking for the question that is going to create the right answer, but the purpose of question is awareness—not answer. And the purpose of choice is awareness—not answer. It's crazy. We contract our awareness to get the right question so we can get the right answer. Yet we get stuck every time we buy an answer. That's the reason everything in Access Consciousness® is about question, question, question—never answer, never conclusion, never "This is the way you want to do it," never "This is what's going to create the result for you." You ask a question to allow the universe to give you awareness.

When you choose to be the question, you become the permeable laws of consciousness. The permeable laws of consciousness hold that when you choose consciousness, it invades other people's realities and their stuck points of view cannot maintain themselves. When you choose consciousness, people have to go into question because consciousness itself is the catalyst for changing what people believe is real that isn't actually real. Choosing consciousness affects and permeates everybody else's universe.

Being you is being all the awareness you are. It's being the question that creates the catalyst, the contribution and the possibilities in other people's worlds by the fact that you are not definable or confinable.

I said this to a friend, and she asked, "Why do I feel so light when you say that?"

I said, "Because you know it's true. You've seen it in action throughout your life. When something is absolutely true, everybody starts to change according to that. When someone is buying a lie, everything gets more solid, more heavy and more difficult. Everybody that comes around you will be altered by you being the permeable laws of consciousness."

Judgment and the Freedom to Choose

In utopian reality, you look beyond what *is* to your idea of what *should be*. You look for the utopian ideal that somebody else has given to you, which means you're in a state of continual judgment. An idealistic or utopian point of view becomes a construct for judging. You think that if you achieve it, you will finally have something, but all you end up with are the limitations you take on by virtue of that judgment. You judge yourself (and everything else around you) against what has or has not been achieved.

This is a problem, because judgment stands in the way of consciousness.

When you're judging, you can't be conscious.

And when you're conscious, there is no judgment in your universe.

In consciousness, everything is included and nothing is judged.

When you include everything and judge nothing, that is consciousness. For example, you may have a construct of what government is supposed to be, and you may want to change the face of government. But if you're going to be conscious, you can't have a judgment about what government does. You've got to realize that government will do what it does because it does what it does. If it's a destructive government, it will do destruction.

Total consciousness in the face of government means that lies will no longer be possible. So, the government can lie to you and you will always know when it is lying. That means you will have greater choice, you will have more awareness and you will be able to choose things other people can't choose because they buy the lies the government tells them.

With a thousand people not having a judgment about what government does and not having a vested outcome in what it does, we could change the face of government.

I want there to be no judgment or no vested interest in anything.

If you can move out of buying into utopian constructs in any way, shape or form, you will see how they create limitation, and you will have a greater freedom to choose. That's the Kingdom of True Choice, where choice becomes an unlimited menu of possibilities. The Kingdom of True Choice is having the willingness to lose all the back doors and all the places you've decided you can't choose from.

When we are in a state of question, multiple choices come up, and every choice creates multiple possibilities. As the possibilities come together, they create a strand of what creates reality for us, and they contribute to the quantum entanglements the universe employs to support us. Quantum entanglements are the string theory that all things are interconnected. It is absolutely true, because if you look at the universe, it's clear that each thing is interconnected with every other thing.

With every question, every choice and every possibility, you're inviting the quantum entanglements of the entire universe to join with you to actualize what you desire. The universe wishes to support us, but we act like we're all alone. It's as if we think the universe is an ecosystem we have to exclude ourselves from. We think we have to do everything ourselves—yet we are part of the whole. If we will embrace ourselves as part of the whole without any judgment, we absolutely invite the whole to be part of us and we open to the universe, which gives us everything we desire.

As long as you have constructs and concepts in place and as long as you function from them, you are not being conscious and you don't have true choice. You are making choices through the limitations of this reality. You're like a horse that's wearing blinders. You can only see straight ahead. You aren't able to look beyond certain parameters because you have bought points of view about the construct of this reality. You create the blinders of your own reality by being unwilling to be aware of everything the universe desires to invite you to. You will try to create within this reality—but you don't want to create *within* this reality. You want to create *beyond* it.

"What Else Is Possible?"

I am always willing to create beyond this reality because I don't see any value in trying to create *within* this reality, *through* this reality or *by* this reality's standards. For me, there is value in asking: What is possible that we have never even considered?

If you are functioning from, "What else is possible?" you are in a state of expansiveness of what can be and what could be. You ask, "How is this choice going to create my life in five years?" You don't go to, "I need to choose the right thing" or "I need to choose to get these people to do or be something different." When you function from, "What else is possible?" a different possibility can show up as if by magic—because it *is* magic.

All the magical things that happen in your life occur because you function from, "What else is possible?" In the moment that you ask that question, you are being the question, and the quantum entanglements of the universe will support you.

True Choice Includes Everything

When you make choices, do you look for a basis from which to choose? The way to tell whether you have a basis from which to choose is to look at the constructs you have bought as true. Maybe you have a basis for choice like, "I am going to have a more expansive life. I am going to get married and have two children, which is the ideal family size, and I am going to live happily ever after behind my white picket fence."

We try to choose based on the correct choice, the right choice, the good choice or the bad choice. *Right choice* is a utopian ideal. We believe correct judgment will lead to the correct choice, and if we choose the right thing, then everything will turn out right, whatever that means. Those are all judgments of choice. They are not a choice of true choice. True choice includes everything. And it judges nothing to determine the choice.

Life on Automatic Pilot

The whole idea of a conceptual construct is that you avoid the need to choose so you can do your life on automatic pilot. That's where you get up in the morning and you don't even choose whether to have coffee or tea. You just put on the kettle and drink whatever happens to fall into your cup. You choose routine in order to eliminate the necessity of choice and awareness. You do routine so everything is predictable and controllable. You don't have to choose anything.

The *military* is a perfect construct because it eliminates all choice in favor of the concept that there is a law, a rule and a structure that will take care of everything for you. You will be fed and clothed, you will know when to get up, you will know when to lie down. You will know everything because it will all be predicted and controlled.

Are you trying to create a predictable life,

instead of a joyful one?

Have you spent your whole life trying to avoid choice? Has everybody told you, "Don't choose the wrong thing. Choose the right thing. That's the wrong choice. You shouldn't have chosen that. Why didn't you choose this other thing?" Everything is predicated on the concept that you must doubt every choice you make, because every choice you make that doesn't fit the conceptual construct of the utopian ideal is a wrong choice.

There Is No Wrong Choice

You have free will—but free will only occurs when you choose. You have to choose! For most people, it's about, "You need to choose what I tell you to choose and if you choose that, you're right."

What you may not realize is there is no wrong choice. When you're in true choice, it's not about making a right or a wrong choice. It's simply, "Okay, what do I want to choose here?"

It's important to recognize that a choice only has to last for ten seconds. It's not the *Lord of the Rings'* one choice to rule them all. It's about choosing—and knowing that a choice is good for about ten seconds. Then you get to choose again. If you choose your life in ten-second increments, you can choose anything. If you don't, you can't.

How many judgments of choice do you have that keep you from having true choice of choice? Choice of choice means just choosing. Just for ten seconds. If what you chose was a great idea in this ten seconds and a bad idea in the next ten seconds, then you can just choose again.

I would like the future to be ever-expanding awareness and consciousness. That's my point of view. But I don't want you to buy my point of view. I don't want you to even consider that my point of view might be the "right" point of view. I want you to look at what's going to work for you. What do you desire? What do you wish to create?

You've got to be willing to be the energy of what creates everything you would like to have, instead of trying to do what's right or what's going to get you what you think the construct of this reality is about.

You may believe there has to be a better version of reality somewhere—and that it exists in conceptual constructs. You may see conceptual constructs as the source for the best of what you have defined as contextual reality. No. The conceptual constructs you have bought into are all the reasons and justifications for the choices you have made to fit, to benefit, to win and to not lose. They totally hem you in to the limitations of this reality. They create the straight jacket that determines what you can choose.

There are so many more possibilities available to us than we realize. But when we function from the constructs of this reality, we are not functioning from something that will contribute to us. We are functioning from something that will work against us. I am asking you to do the one thing that nobody else in the world will ask of you—and that is to choose you, to be you and to show up as you, because you are the best thing that ever happened.

> What physical actualization of a future of total choice are you now capable of generating, creating and instituting? Everything that doesn't allow that to show up times a godzillion, will you destroy and uncreate it all? Right and wrong, good and bad, POC and POD, all 9, shorts, boys and beyonds.

> *What do you want to choose?*

Systems vs Structures

I was talking with my son recently, and he said, "The police is a system that's really ugly."

I said, "No, it's not a system. It's a structure. A system is something that is malleable and changeable. It can be adjusted according to the moment. A structure is something you put in place that has laws, regulations and rules that you have to follow. The military is a structure; it's not a system. The law is a structure; it's not a system.

A system adapts to what you want. Access Consciousness® is a system. We don't have rigid rules. Access adjusts according to the moment and the people in it. When we have a class, I'm not trying to present a structure that will allow people to go to a certain place. I'm asking the people to be present in a way that leads us to new places. I ask of every person who comes to class: Be in the space where new places and spaces can be accessed. It's a system—not a structure. Rules are few and far between.

The system is like the question. It's like the choice. It's like the possibility. It allows the quantum entanglements to contribute to you, while a structure eliminates anything but the "right" point of view. There are a whole lot of structures out there but very few systems. Accounting programs are a structure. The IRS is a structure.

There are a lot of people who are saying, "Use my system and you will succeed," but what they're offering is not a system. They are attempting to sell their structure as though it's a system that will adapt to your needs—but unfortunately you will only get a result if you do things their way. They're calling it a system, but it's not. It's a structure. A system is always malleable, changeable and adaptable to the moment.

In my life, my system is being the question. A contractor who is doing some work on my house called me this morning in a meltdown. She said, "This occurred, this occurred and this occurred."

I asked, "So, what could you do different that would create a different possibility?"

She said, "Oh! I can do this, this and this!"

That one little question opened the door for her to see everything from a different place, and within five minutes, she was out of the stew she had been in. A system puts a question foremost in your mind as the doorway to options and possibilities you haven't considered.

Choice Is Creation

Nothing happens to you. You make everything in your life occur the way it does. So, if you're not happy with the way your life is showing up, instead of saying, "Such-and-such happened to me," you might want to look at what else you could do, what else you could be, what else you could create or what else you could generate—because choice is creation.

You create everything that happens in your life. It's all your creation, but you may not be willing to lose the place in which you are the effect of something, where things "just happen" and you're an innocent bystander in your life. You may act innocent, but I know you aren't. You're a perpetrator of magnitude against you.

Necessity and No Choice

You keep talking about experience as though what you experience occurs because you have no choice or because a choice has been made for you, rather than asking, "What am I creating here that I haven't even considered?" It's as if you don't believe in choice. You think you have to do things. You think necessity is real. Anything you have made a necessity becomes a place where no choice can exist. When you function from the no-choice universe, all you're doing is proving the rightness of your point of view that the only way to choose for you is to choose against someone else.

Are you willing to lose the no-choice universe?

Effort and Creation

You may also not believe in creation. You may believe things are created through effort and that exerting effort proves you are accomplishing something. Only if an activity takes effort do you feel you have accomplished anything. Only with effort is something created. If something happens instantaneously and there is no effort involved, you say, "It happened to me."

No. It didn't just happen. You created it. You are capable of instantaneous actualization. Why will you not acknowledge this? In the metaphysical community, people talk about manifestation. That's not what I'm talking about. If you look up the word *manifestation*, you'll see that it means *how* something shows up—not *that* it shows up. Actualization is *that* it shows up. You have to look at what you are actualizing and bringing into reality. You have to look at what you are creating—because choice is creation.

Functioning from the Choice

The utopian ideal is, "If I take this construct and apply it to my life, my life will be perfect." I have a friend who didn't want her life to be perfect. She already had that. What she wanted was a life that was beyond everything else she saw—beyond the limitations of this reality that everybody else lived from.

I said to her, "If you're really going to live outside of this reality, you've got to be out of control, out of definition, out of limitation, out of form, structure and significance, out of linearity and out of concentricities. That means you're no longer trying to fit into this reality. You're willing to create a reality that has more possibilities in it. When you're doing that, you're operating outside of structures. You are creating a system."

She said, "Yes, that's what I've been looking for." That was her knowing. That was not utopia. That can't become a construct because it's functioning from true choice, and when you're functioning from true choice, nothing can be put into a construct. What you want is a life that is beyond everything else you see and beyond the limitations everybody else lives from. There is no wrong choice, because if you're in true choice, it's not about a right or wrong choice. It's "Okay, what do I want to choose here and now?"

Is this going to be difficult? Yes, because you have to learn to choose. You've spent your whole life trying to avoid choice. Everybody has told you, "No, no. Don't choose that. You've got to choose the right thing. That's the wrong choice. You shouldn't have chosen that. Why didn't you choose this other thing?" Everything is predicated on the idea that you must doubt every choice you made, because every choice you made that didn't fit the conceptual construct of the utopian ideal was a wrong choice.

There Are No Reasons

People often try to prove their choices are "right" by finding the "reason" they made the choice. They say, "I chose this because ____." No. There is no reason you chose it. You just chose it.

True choice is simply "I chose this."

You keep trying to go for reasons. You say, "The reason for this is ____. The reason for that is ____." There is no reason for anything. There is just choice. Choice creates what shows up in your life. All choice creates. Good choice creates. Bad choice creates. Stupid choice creates. Everything that shows up in your life is based on what you have created, good, bad, smart, stupid, beautiful, or ugly. So the question is, "What would you like to choose?"

Do you ever say, "I'm so upset because ____"? *Because* has no relevance. You are upset. Why is that your choice? Why do you choose upset? The primary reason for choosing upset is to make other people wrong. It's sort of like cutting your wrists so that somebody will notice that you're committing suicide.

The person says, "Hi. You're bleeding."

You say, "Yes I know."

The person says, "Oh I'm sorry. Would you like a Band-Aid?"

You say, "No."

The person says, "But you're bleeding. Wouldn't you like a Band-Aid?"

You say, "No. I'm bleeding."

The person says, "Oh, okay, 'bye."

You call out, "Can't you see that I'm bleeding? Why aren't you reacting the way you're supposed to?"

I recently heard a joke: There's a group of bikers riding along, going over a big bridge. One of the bikers, a tough guy in a leather jacket and boots, sees a beautiful woman on the ledge about to jump off the bridge. He stops and asks, "What are you doing?"

She says, "I'm going to jump."

He says, "But you're beautiful. Why don't you come down and give me a kiss before you jump?"

So she goes down and gives him a big kiss.

All You've Got to Do Is Choose

I was talking with a thirteen-year-old girl who has been coming to Access Consciousness® classes since she was five years old. She was one of the kids who asked me, "Can't we have a class just for kids? These adults are so slow."

I asked her, "What do you see here that the adults won't choose?"

She said, "They always say they are going to let something go, but then they change their mind and they don't do it. They keep asking the same question over and over again, year after year. It's like they are stuck on a treadmill."

You're on a treadmill of "I will, but I won't." You have a choice and you don't choose. A kid looks at you and says, "All you've got to do is choose." You keep talking about your choice as though eventually you will choose it, yet you never do. A thirteen-year-old girl has been watching you not choosing for eight years. She wonders what's wrong with you.

It's your life. It's your reality. Do you like it the way it is?

Or do you want to change it?

If you want to change it, choose.

Choice in this reality has been about choosing to not be disliked, not be judged, not live too different, not to stand out from the crowd. It's about choosing *not*, choosing *not*, choosing *not*. Ninety percent of what's being created right now is choosing *not*; it's not about choosing *to*.

I see the power and the potency that you could be, and I would like you to be the miracle you are. I would like you to be so much more than you have been willing to be—and it is far greater than anything you have imagined was possible. There is so much more that you could choose. There is so much more that you could be. All you have to do is choose it.

Your Choice Will Change Reality

If you are like most people, you have spent your life trying to choose from the menu of this reality. The menu of this reality is: You're right, you're wrong, you're good, you're bad, you're limited, you're not limited. None of it is about what is actually possible that you haven't even considered.

I don't look at anything from rightness or wrongness or good or bad. Whatever the choice is, I always look at "What is this going to create? How is this choice going to create a different possibility? How is this choice going to create a different possibility that I haven't even considered is possible?"

What if you looked at your choices from that point of view? What if you started to create from what is possible that you never even considered? I always do. When I'm looking at a choice, I never ask, "How is this going to work in this reality?" I ask, "What is this going to create that's beyond anything I have ever known, anything I have ever thought was possible, anything that will create something greater than what has actually been on planet Earth so far?"

Your choice will change reality. Please get this. The Kingdom of True Choice is recognizing that everything you choose creates a different world. Want to create a different world? Then choose. Stop pretending that your choice has no relevance. Your choice from the state of consciousness will create a change in everybody else's realities.

Is that what you would like to create? Then choose it!

People have always known they are special. They think, "I must be special, I must be special, I must be special," but they don't actually *claim* it. I always knew I was special too, but nobody else saw it, so I negated it. I wanted a different reality, but no one else could see that reality, so I denied it. I knew there was something I could do that could create a change for the world, but I couldn't find it—because I was looking in everybody else's pocket for value, rather than in my own pocket.

Each of us, as the gift we are, has something to offer that could change everything. You have to look in your own pocket to find the gift that's been there your whole life. You know it's there. You know you have it. But instead of claiming it, you always look into someone else's reality, trying to find something of value there.

You are a unique gift to the world. Do you ever acknowledge that? What would it take for you to acknowledge what you are, what you're capable of, and what you have not yet chosen, that if you would choose it, would change everything?

How many choices that are available to you are you not

acknowledging, that if you would acknowledge them,

would change the world to what you'd like it to be?

Scan for more information

◊

DOING SOMETHING DIFFERENT

I look at somebody who has an illness and I ask, "What is this?"

They have a giant elephant standing behind them, pooping on their head. They say, "I've got so much elephant poop on my head, I can't see." Why don't they move out from under the elephant? That would be my question.

I say, "If you move three feet to the right, the elephant can't poop on you."

They say, "Yes, but that won't work. I can't move. I've got too much elephant poop around me."

If I were sitting under an elephant that was pooping on me, I'd say, "This is not working. I've got too much elephant poop on my head. Now, what can I do different? Oh, I could take a shower. Now all the elephant poop is gone. That's so much better!"

Are You Interested in Total Difference?

Once when Dain and I were talking about a situation in his life that wasn't working, I asked him, "What are you going to do different?"

Dain said, "I don't want to do something different. I just want to change the situation."

I asked, "What do you mean? Why wouldn't you choose something different?"

He said, "Because I've got to fix this situation."

I said, "What? That's not the way people function. If people knew they could do something different, wouldn't they do something different?"

Dain said, "No, they'd just change what wasn't working."

That brief conversation changed my whole reality and it changed all of Access Consciousness®—because I had created Access with the idea that if people knew they could choose something different, they wouldn't try to fix a situation that wasn't working. Everything I created in Access Consciousness® was based on the idea that they would choose different.

Recently I was having stomach trouble. I kept trying various things and they made my stomach somewhat better, but they didn't take the trouble away. I asked, "What am I doing here?" I realized that I was trying to change the situation; I was not trying to do something different. You may be doing this as well. You're trying to change what isn't working, as though that's going to make it work for you. You think, "If I can just make this work, then everything will be okay."

You are willing to change something you've decided needs to be changed, but you are not willing to do or be something different that would completely eliminate the situation that's not working. You want a slightly different result—but only slightly. You're not interested in total difference.

I talked with my friends, Steve and Chutisa Bowman, about their consulting business. They work with businesses and organizations around the world, and they give people all kinds amazing ideas. Steve said, "I don't understand why people take one piece of what we suggest and try to fit it into what they've already got, instead of creating something entirely different."

I said, "Those people are configurators. They configure things; they take one piece of information and try to fit it into the slots of all the things they have already decided are true and real. They don't change anything and they don't do anything different. They just try to make the idea you gave them another tool in the toolbox of how they keep their reality going the way it's going." That's continually fixing the broken-down car, rather than getting a different one.

Configurators are different from extrapolators. Extrapolators are people who see ten different possibilities; they get ten different images of something that's possible, and they say, "If I take this one over here on the right, and this one on the left, and this one in the middle, and this one on the not-so-far right, and put them all together, I can create something different." Extrapolation is the way progress occurs. Extrapolators create the most change and the most possibility. Steve Jobs was an extrapolator. Is his company as viable now that he's gone? No, because they don't have an extrapolator in charge any more. They have a configurator who is trying to put everything into the same structure he believed Jobs created—except it wasn't a structure at all. It was a system.

An extrapolator will hear a great new idea and say, "Wow. What can I create that I haven't considered?" and something else comes into existence. We have not been encouraged to extrapolate and come up with something that didn't exist before. Instead, we have been taught to get it right. We have been trained to do what other people do, and to simply do it better. We have been told to buy a structure or a system that has worked for somebody else—none of which has anything to do with true choice, true creation, true generation, or true possibilities.

Different vs Differently

You haven't been willing to be something different, do something different, and have something different. If you truly wish to create something different, you have to do it from a different position. It's not about doing the same thing *differently*—it's about doing something *different*. *Differently* is sort of changing it. *Different* is another universe. Doing something different creates the place where you can go beyond changing it. You are willing to eliminate and lose what you're trying to change.

People often say to me, "I want to change this."

I say, "Okay, so lose it."

They ask, "Well, if I lose it, what will happen?"

I say, "What? If you really want to change it, lose it."

They say, "No. You've got to explain to me why I would want to lose it."

I say, "Because it will create a completely different reality."

They say, "Yeah, but I'm not sure I want to lose it."

They are not willing to go with, "I have no idea what it's going to look like, but I'm going to have a totally different reality." They want change to a degree; they don't want to lose what has been holding in place everything that limits them. They don't really want a different reality. They simply want to alter what they have going on. They just want to experience it *differently*, so they try to make a small change they have decided is acceptable. I am talking about total *difference*. They are talking about changing something somewhat. Most people would rather be functional in this reality than function from a totally different reality.

When I was a young man, I saved up a bunch of money and went to Europe for six months. When I started out, I tried to re-establish who I was every day based on the way I had defined myself in the past After the first two weeks, I realized nobody knew me as any of things I used to be, so I could invent myself each day instead of trying to live by who I had decided I was. That was a huge shift and change.

I bought a car and I began to have all kinds of adventures. I would go to the American Express office in a city, and people would be there, holding a sign, "Will pay for gas money to go to ____". I'd pick up somebody that I'd never met before and I'd travel with them for a short while. Then I'd do that again with someone else. All kinds of curious and amazing things happened on those trips.

Most of us don't give ourselves a place where we can be or do different. We function from "I'm my kid's father, I'm my father's son, I'm my dog's owner, I'm my job's person," or however we have defined ourselves. What I'm talking about is living in a sense of curiosity about who and what you're going to be today, what you're going to create today, and where you're going to be today. It's "Who am I today and what grand and glorious adventure am I going to have?"

Unfortunately, most people wake up in the morning and think, "What do I have to do today?" That's not a question—and it's not creating grand and glorious adventures. When I got the tool, "Who am I today and what grand and glorious adventure am I going to have?" I began to use it every day, and I noticed that my reality became a place where something new was continuously generated because of the difference in my point of view.

We have learned to build barriers and to not receive in order to function within the structures we've decided we have to be or do in order to live with the people we have decided we have to have in our life. Those, by the way, are the people that own us. They're the ones we think we have to be or do things for.

What Can You Do or Be Different?

You cut off your awareness of you in order to live in this reality. So, what can you do or be different?

You could try being vulnerable. Vulnerability is the willingness to have no scab on the wound of being. You don't build barriers to what you're aware of and what you can receive. You're willing to receive everything with no point of view. There's a level of sensitivity, and the intensity of the information you receive is dynamically exponentialized.

We keep trying to scab over our awareness so it's less intense. We think that if we can ease off the intensity of awareness, we will be able to handle it better. That's what we've been taught to do. As kids, when we were intensely aware, our parents would tell us, "You can't know that. You can't have that. That can't be right." We would say, "Uh, okay, I guess I can't."

Total vulnerability is total receiving. If you're totally willing to receive, then you won't cut off any awareness you have of you or about you.

> What can you be or do different, that if you would be or do it different, would allow you to eliminate, eradicate, and lose everything you would like to change? Everything that is times a godzillion, will you destroy and uncreate it all? Right and wrong, good and bad, POC and POD, all 9, shorts, boys, and beyonds.

> *What can you be or do different,*
>
> *that if you would be or do it different,*
>
> *would allow you to eliminate, eradicate,*
>
> *and lose your resistance to your own awareness?*
>
> *Now that's doing and being different!*

Creation Through Anguish

Are you one of those people who isn't willing to choose something different until you're in anguish? Anguish is a turbulent sense of discomfort so intensely awful that it feels like you're going to die if you have to keep experiencing it. Only when you're in anguish will you do something different. Only when you have anguish are you willing to choose something dynamically.

It's the anguish of business. It's the anguish of what could go wrong that you have to prepare for so you can handle it. It's the anguish of owning property. It's the anguish of having too much. It's the anguish of not having a relationship. You think you're going to get out of the anguish of not having a relationship by having one. Then you get one and you ask, "Why the hell did I choose this?" But instead of choosing something different, you stay with it for years until the anguish is so horrible you finally get divorced. Until the anguish is bad enough, you won't do anything different.

It's creation through anguish. It's the belief that creation occurs only when you have anguish, lack, and need. You will not create without those elements. Until you come to the conclusion that you're in anguish, you won't change anything. You say, "My life is okay."

I love that one. Really? Your life is okay? Could you let your face know?

"I'm happy."

Really? That's your happy face? If that's your happy face, I'm scared.

Some people are better at creating a happy face than others. They say, "Can't you see how happy I am? I'm so happy. Look at how happy I am."

I reply, "You don't look happy. You look insane."

People often try to solidify depression into existence. They try to make depression real—but it's not real. It's just a choice. Is this something you do? Instead of choosing, you try to solidify things into existence, which will create anguish, which will then create change.

You may not realize that you don't just automatically have a point of view. Your point of view is a choice. You choose to have the points of view you have—and those choices create your reality. Every time you choose a point of view, you create a potential future. You create the quantum entanglements that create a future based on the choice you made to have that point of view.

Sometimes when people express a point of view, I ask, "What's the value of that point of view?"

They say, "It's mine and I'm keeping it. So there!"

I'm trying to show you what you're choosing. When something is not creating what you would like to create, your anguish is not going to create something different. But your choice will. When you recognize that something is not working, you have to go to choice.

"This doesn't work for me," is the awareness that you have suffered as much anguish as you're going to suffer. You recognize that anguish is not what you want to choose. Only then will you go to question and choice. Only then will you ask, "What could I do different? What other choices do I have here?"

> What anguish are you using to suppress the choices of joy you could be choosing if nothing were missing and nothing were needed in any reality? Everything that is times a godzillion, will you destroy and uncreate it all? Right and wrong, good and bad, POC and POD, all 9, shorts, boys, and beyonds.

The People You Choose

You may be like the people on the Golden Planet. We assumed that the techies, who actually had nothing to offer and simply wanted our gold, were greater than we were.

You may think the people around you are so brilliant and essential to you that you hold onto them for dear life when they are actually costing you your life and your living. This is not assisting you in generating and creating the life you are capable of.

Or you may choose people who are limited enough that you can control them. You may think that's the way to create what you're trying to create. When you do this, you don't seem to take into account that what you're trying to create won't be any greater than what you have created before. If you want to create something that's greater than what you've ever created before, you've got to choose people who will not live with limitation but will demand of you that you be greater and demand of themselves that they be greater.

Please look at the people you choose to be with and see whether they expand your life. Generally speaking, because of the utopian ideals you buy, you tend to choose people who never make you go beyond the limitations of where you currently exist. You choose people to have relationships with, people to have friendships with, and people to have sex with because they will buy into the utopian construct of your ideal scene. They will never demand of you that you go beyond your limitations.

How can you screw yourself up more than by choosing the people you choose? It doesn't have to be this way when you are willing to look at possibilities, choices, questions, and contribution—because all of a sudden, you will realize, "This person is not a sufficient contribution to my life. This person is contributing to my control, limitation, maintenance, and contraction. This relationship is not creating what I'd like to create." Once you realize this, you can choose not to do that anymore.

Choose People Who Contribute to the Greatness of You

I invite you to choose people who contribute to the greatness of you, not people who make you less. I invite you not to let the people who are trying to find the rightness of their point of view and the wrongness of yours even come close to your reality. I encourage you to recognize, "That person doesn't mean anything to me. Bye-bye."

In your business, are you choosing people who are less than you in order to make you feel more of you? Are you making sure that you have the one person that you can control, maintain, contract, and limit without question or change? What if you chose people who would demand that you be more of you at all times? Have you ever hired somebody who would make you step up? No? Maybe it's time to do that.

You have to choose people to be on your team who are willing to be stars in their own right. You have to not control them, not do everything for them, and not get them to ask you everything. You just have to get them to be aware in their own right of what they're capable of.

"I Hired You for Your Awareness"

At one point, Blossom, our Project Manager for Access Consciousness®, researched something for me. She came over and said, "You have these choices: this choice, this choice, or this choice."

I said, "I don't want you to give me choices. I want you to give me your awareness of what you think is the best choice. Then I will tell you *yes* or *no*. I didn't hire you for your ability to analyze. I hired you for your awareness."

She said, "Oh! This is what we should do," which was a whole lot easier than going through the things she was trying to get me to choose from that I didn't really care about.

The one thing I know about Blossom is she'll look at the easiest and best possibility. That's how she functions in life. She will look from a place of awareness to determine what's going to work the best for what we're trying to accomplish, and she will do this without making a judgment. It's the awareness I want, not her judgment. You've got to look at how people function—and choose people who function from awareness. When you make it about the person's awareness, they have to maintain their creative capacity. They can't just check out and go away. I never let anybody check out and go away.

What conceptual construct of the utopian ideal of separation are you using to control, maintain, contract, and limit the people you are choosing? Everything that is times a godzillion, will you destroy and uncreate it all? Right and wrong, good and bad, POC and POD, all 9, shorts, boys, and beyonds.

Becoming Useless

Most people try to make themselves useful. They want to prove they have value. That's their hierarchy of value: Whoever is useful is valuable.

What's the one thing that, from your point of view, makes you most useful in your job? You may think it's your ability to solve any problem. If you believe that, what do you have to create in order to prove that you are valuable and useful? Problems! You need to take a look at this, because being useful is probably not in your best interest.

I have become totally useless. I've done everything I could to get all the people I work with to the point where they don't need my input at all. Once I'd done that, I said, "Wow, they don't ask me things any more. They used to ask me about stuff. Now I am totally useless. I must be old. I'd better retire."

Then I said, "Screw that. I'm out-creating them." That opened the door for me to create something greater. Now I am out-creating things in the business so they have to look from a different place. They have to step up to a bigger game as a result of my willingness to be useless. That has opened the door for me to create something greater, and for them to be as great as they can be.

If you truly want your business to grow, you've got to get to the point where you're useless; however, you may be unwilling to lose your usefulness. If you work yourself out of a job, what do you do? Do you retire? Or do you create and generate something greater? If you're a humanoid, you'll want to create and generate something greater. But if you're not willing to be useless, you will never out-create what your business is today; you will only re-create what you did yesterday.

It's helpful to know that there are two species of two-legged beings on this planet. We call them humans and humanoids. They look alike, they walk alike, they talk alike, and they often eat alike, but the reality is they're different. Humans will always tell you how you're wrong, how they're right, and how you shouldn't change anything. They say things like, "We don't do things that way, so don't even bother." They are the ones who ask, "Why are you changing that? It's fine the way it is."

Humanoids take a different approach. They are always looking at things and asking, "How can we change that? What will make this better? How can we outdo this?" They're the people who have created all the great art, all the great literature, and all the great progress on the planet. You need to recognize whether you are a human or a humanoid. If you're reading this book and you've gotten this far, there's a 99.99999% chance that you're a humanoid. You wish to create and generate something greater—so you'll need to become willing to be useless and to choose people who also wish to create something greater.

What if you became useless as a problem solver?

Being the Source, the Catalyst, the Contribution and the Possibility

A utopia is a place where everything is ideal and everything can be defined. Utopian constructs are all designed to create an answer, which you then perpetrate on the rest of the world in order to impel them to choose the construct you've bought into rather than some other one. Somewhere in life you have determined that you need a particular construct or you will never achieve the utopian ideal where everybody is happy and everybody is equal.

Are You Making Yourself the Source?

Do you have to take care of everything and everyone in your business, your relationships, your family, and your life? If so, you are making yourself the source. If you make yourself the source, everybody has to turn to you, and you have to take care of them. Are you good at taking care of everybody? Do you like taking care of them? Or do you want to stomp them to death when they want you to take care of them?

Being a source is a conclusion and it's also an awareness. You are a source. That's true. But when you conclude that you *are* the source or *must* be the source, you create limitation. You're buying into the utopian ideal that when you come to the right answer, you will finally know. You need to be more than the source. You need to be able to be the source, the contribution, the catalyst, and the possibility. If you are willing to be those four elements, you'll know, "Okay, right now what I need to be is a catalyst, not a source" or "Now I need to be a contribution" or "I need to be a possibility these people haven't even considered." You become all of these creative elements, instead of just one.

Working with People

When you work with people, you want to be a catalyst, a possibility, or a choice for change, not the source for change. If you're the source for change, you have to make all the decisions. That's not what you want. You want people to be able to contribute to you—and they can't do that if you're the source for all answers. You have to be the catalyst for getting people to look at possibilities instead of getting them to look to you as the source. You have to be able to create a catalytic response in people.

If a molecule is left alone, it will maintain the constancy of its structure. Science tells us that if we, as beings, look at a molecule, we change it by virtue of observing it. That's because we are an energy that is a contribution and a catalyst to changing the way it looks and the way it functions. We need to recognize that we have that level of power and learn how to use it. We are also the source for what catalyzes the molecular structure of things.

When you see a wrongness, you are looking at the negative, so you've got to ask, "What change is available here?" That is the positive charge, which will create movement in the electronic system of the nucleus of you. When you do this, you activate the catalyzing effect that you can be in the world. You are the catalyst for a different possibility if you are willing to be that. It's a choice you can make.

Healing

You can be a catalyst for healing, you can be a source for healing, you can be a contribution to healing, or you can be a possibility of healing. Which one sticks you in place and limits you? Being the source.

Healing is a capacity you have, but you keep trying to look for the ideal version of it, in which it is defined in a particular way. Many people think that healing requires them to take on illness, pain, limitation, or problem into their body, so that in an ideal scene, under an ideal condition, they would remove everything from another person's body and the person would be healed the way Jesus did it.

But healing has many different aspects. There are people who do art and who heal with their art. There are people who touch others and heal them. There are people who create music and heal. There is kindness, which is healing. There are thousands of ways in which healing exists, but none of those have been idealized because those kinds of healing are not utopian concepts.

When you have to be the source of healing, you eliminate the contribution. You limit things that would change a lot of realities. Whenever you are the source for healing, you lock the pain, illness, or whatever it is into your body, but the other person does not actually release it. The other person can only be healed if you are around and you continue to take the pain or illness from them. They will not see that they are a contribution to healing their own body. They also have to recognize that they are a contribution to the choice they made to be ill. So, don't try to be the source for healing. You've got to be willing to be the catalyst.

I ran one of our new processes with my son. We were talking on the phone and he was saying, "Ugh, I'm sick. I'm always sick."

I asked, "So, what are you sick of, son?"

He said, "I'm sick of this with my girlfriend."

"Okay, what else are you sick of?"

"I'm sick of this with my daughter."

"What else are you sick of?"

He named about twelve different things he was sick of.

I said, "Well, I hope you feel better," and I hung up. I didn't say anything. I didn't POC and POD* him. I just asked him what he was sick of.

---

* POC and POD are defined at the end of the book in the section on The Clearing Statement.

The next day, I called him and asked, "How are you doing?"

"I'm great!"

"Good. Not sick anymore?"

"Sick? Was I sick?"

When you create that level of change, the person can't remember how it used to be because his reality is changed. That's the kind of catalyst you want to be.

Facilitating People Through Access Consciousness® Processing

When you are facilitating someone through Access Consciousness® processing, the client is the source of change or no change. The question is the catalyst. You are the possibility, which is why the client came to you. Your clients are looking for something that they have found impossible. You have shown them that there is possibility. You exude the element called possibility. This is ultimately catalyst and contribution.

If you see yourself as the source, then you always have to be wrong when you don't succeed in giving them the change you have decided they should have. I never decide what someone should have. I just ask, "What can I do for you today?"

Sometimes you can't change things you think are important to change. Sometimes you have to wait until there is a moment that is appropriate for the person to choose to change.

"What is this?" is the source.

"What do I do with it?" is the possibility.

"Can I change it?" is the question.

"If so, how do I change it?" is the catalyst. The catalyst is always a contribution that the quantum entanglements support.

The more you choose consciousness, the more you will permeate people's reality and the less they will be willing to hold on to their limitations. Consciousness supports those who choose consciousness, and when you are willing to be the permeable laws of consciousness, it actualizes as a different reality. You become a catalyst for change because by being you, you change everybody around you.

Scan for more information

◊

CREATING YOUR LIFE/CREATING YOUR FUTURE

How do you create your life and your future?

You create it with question, possibility, choice, and contribution.

Rather than using these four elements,

most people look for the ideal situation

and come to conclusions and decisions about what it should be.

Future Is About Awareness

Before the techies arrived on the Golden Planet, there were no movies. We didn't need to see pictures of actors on a screen getting emotional about things. The entire universe was our theater of living. We lived with every molecule in existence and enjoyed it. We got to hear it, see it, experience it, and feel it. Everything was there for us all the time. We had the sense that we were always full.

When the techies came with their technical capacity, we bought the idea that we needed technology, including movies. We decided the techies' utopian ideals would give us more than what we already had, a mistake that was both tragic and ironic, and we ended up where we are right now, with the sense that we are always empty.

We believe we will have what we desire in the future if we take on a concept or a utopian ideal. We use utopian constructs as though things are going to come out the way we have decided they should come out. We create a conceptual construct of what we think the future should be. Then we head for that. We say, "That mountain over there is the future, so that's where I'm going." When we get to the mountain, we say, "Oh. I thought this was the future. Now look at how many mountains are beyond it." Then we create another concept. "That must be where the future is, and I'm going there."

Instead of looking at the actual moment we're in and enjoying that and being grateful for the fact that we have that moment, we say things like "In the future, we will *(fill in the blank)*. We will have children. We will have a white picket fence. We will have the perfect house." We're always looking for another place to go, another space to be, and another place to belong. We do the same thing with our business. "When my business gets off the ground, it will be *(fill in the blank)*." We try to create based on utopian conceptual constructs, rather than asking, "What about the future am I aware of that I haven't considered yet?"

You don't realize that most of the sayings and slogans you live by are conceptual constructs. When you choose to live by conceptual constructs, you pay the price with your awareness. You maintain your conceptual constructs by reducing your awareness.

You may have a conceptual construct of the future you have decided will come to fruition tomorrow. That's not future. The future is not a conceptual construct; future is not about completion, and it's not about getting it the way you want it. Future is about awareness. If you desire a future based on awareness and true choice, you have to create from a level of consciousness and communion with the universe.

> What conceptual construction of the utopian ideal of separation are you using to control, maintain, contract, and limit your future? Everything that is times a godzillion, will you destroy and uncreate it all? Right and wrong, good and bad, POC and POD, all 9, shorts, boys, and beyonds.

Definition, by Definition Alone, Is Limitation

Once when I was working with a group of people, I asked, "What percentage of you are you not choosing?"

Somebody said, "Nine hundred ninety percent," and it exactly matched the energy. I knew that was totally correct.

I said, "Wow!" We're only using ten percent of who we actually are to live in this physical reality. What if we would live from the other 990%? What could get created under those circumstances? What might we be able to do or be that we've never shown anyone we could do or be?"

I'm talking about those magic moments in your life when you got some place too fast or you suddenly had something show up that had been missing forever and which you found in some place it couldn't have been. Are those the real capacities we have? Yes. Why are we not using and being those instead of making our lives about the linear construct of time and "I will find it eventually" or "I will get there eventually"? What if there was no "eventually"? What if there was only simultaneity and instantaneity?

Since then I have often talked about how most folks settle for about ten percent of what's possible in their lives rather than going for 990% of what's possible, and I never understood why people didn't get it. It is so obvious to me. I am so willing to go beyond the ten percent, yet I notice that other people are not able or willing to do that. Occasionally they will zip up to fifteen percent and they undo it ten minutes later.

Then I realized it has to do with constructs. People limit themselves with the conceptual constructs they buy into. One of these is the concept of future. They attempt to define what the future is going to be—but definition, by definition alone, is limitation. Whenever you attempt to define anything, you contract your awareness and you stifle the growth of the thing you've defined. When you function from the ideal, you believe you must define the future—or you can't have it. You define the limitations you will function from to get to the future you've decided is ideal, which is a future that can't exist.

We limit and contract ourselves with all kinds of definitions. A while ago, Dain told me he hadn't been having that much fun doing his sessions. I looked at it and asked, "Have you contracted what you do in order to meet the definition of Energetic Synthesis of Being that you created?"

He said, "Yes." He had been trying to contract what he was doing with Energetic Synthesis of Being so he could give that to people, when what he actually needed to do was to be the source for creating a different future by being the curiosity of possibilities and choice. It's not about defining the future with constructs and contracting yourself to create the solidification of the future that you see or the future you have decided ought to be as a greater version of what you currently have. You need to choose from the question, "What is the future that will be created 1,000 years from now by the choice I make today?"

Notice you can't solidify that.

Dain is now changing what he does with his sessions because he saw that he had been trying to get people to *choose* to be. What he's got to do is get them to choose. He has chosen to change what he does to the Symphony of Possibilities. That's orchestrating all the molecular structures of the universe to create a different possibility than you've ever been willing to have before. The results he has been getting are phenomenal.

Whenever you try to get anything right, whenever you try to see things from any point of view, you solidify it. You limit it. For example, you may say, "What I want for my future is to make a million dollars." What if a million dollars is a limitation of your life, not the possibility of it? What if there is something greater than what you have ever considered?

Without the walls of this reality, everything would be expansive, and you would be in a constant state of possibility, choice, and question—not a place where you're trying to define what you want to create, what you want to do, what you want to generate, how you want it to look, or any of that.

When you function from oneness and consciousness, there is no definition of future. You don't solidify the future; you permeate it. You actually create the space of future. It's a different way of functioning.

Do you want a future that has a primary motivation

of expansion—

or do you want a predictable future?

The Future Is Not Solid

The future doesn't have solidity like the past or the present, yet we keep trying to solidify what we would like to create as a future. We think that's the way to bring it into existence. The problem with this approach is that it takes the future out of question and puts it into the structure of this reality, which requires us to put massive amounts of energy into it in order to create it.

Often you are not comfortable looking at the future because the future is too much space and not enough solidity. So, you try to create a solidity of the future by contracting your awareness. You start to create something that's space, and then you choose something that solidifies it and makes it feel like what you are used to having. You try to solidify it back into that more familiar position. The positions that you function from are always designed in your own universe, in your own head. You design them as though they are going to create what you want. They don't!

You may have a stable point in existence, where you have your past and your present, and you may try to align your future with these, so it will be a stable point as well. As soon as you get out of that solid comfort zone, you begin to look for something to bring you back to your comfortable middle ground. It's almost like you're a pendulum. That stable point might feel comfortable to you, but it's the way you create separation between you, yourself, and your future. If you separate you from you, if you separate you from others, you also separate you from your awareness of the future. Whatever position you wish to keep in place becomes the limit of what your future can be. I try to keep nothing in place; therefore, I am always able to change things.

Seeking the Missing Element

I have seen a number of people decide they wish to create Access Consciousness® classes. They put out energy, put out energy, put out energy, and all of a sudden they start to create Access Consciousness® classes. Then they go into confusion. They want to have more of what they have created, but they don't know how to have that. They ask, "In order to have more of what I created, do I have to put out more energy? Or do I have to put out less energy? Or do I have to change something?"

They may think they're asking questions, but actually they are trying to come to conclusion. They are seeking the missing element as though the missing element is going to make the future solid.

They want a more expansive future. They want more people coming to classes. They want more people coming to consciousness. They want more things going on in their lives, but they aren't creating and generating those things. They might get a totally different result if they asked, "What, if I institute it today, would create a different reality in five years?"

Feel the energy of that question. Use it in your life.

Solidifying the Future

When you try to create your future from a solid point of view, you're attempting to match it with something solid from the past or the present. Some people do repetitive action as though that is going to create the result they desire. Others try to make the future solid by using their minds to create what they want. That's a difficulty, because they try to think themselves into something, believing that's the motion that is necessary. It's not.

This way of operating is based on the sense that you are missing something in your life, which keeps you from being what you actually are and seeing the future that you seek. Every time you look at a future of expansive possibility, you feel a sense of space, and then you try to fill it up with something.

People who hoard do this. They can't stand the sense of space. They have to fill in all the spaces around them with stuff so they know they have a solid reality—until finally they become overwhelmed with the level of solidity they have created. They have no way of creating space—and space (not solidity) is what they need to create the future.

Forecasting the Future vs Forecasting Possibilities

Forecasting the future is another way of limiting it. It is casting your future in front of you as though it is something solid that will be waiting for you when you get there. You seem to think you have to create something that's very solid in order to make it a reality. That's not how it works. You future is something you create with your choices.

There is, however, a great use for forecasting. It's forecasting possibilities. Forecasting possibilities means you're willing to look at the future and see what your choice is going to create. This is different from trying to solidify into existence the thing you have decided you want. Forecasting possibilities is about sensing. It's an awareness. I call it seeing because it's a level of awareness that is greater than the reality you have been taught to perceive.

Many years ago, when I was trying to figure out what my future was going to be, I used to go to psychics, thinking they could see the future I couldn't see. After a certain level of doing Access Consciousness®, I discovered I had no solid future. And whenever the psychics would try to do a reading for me, they'd read about my children, my ex-wife, or someone else in my life, but they could never read about me. I began to realize I was no longer casting my desire for future into the future to find a place I could anchor myself. My future wasn't readable. They couldn't foresee it. They couldn't forecast it because it wasn't solid.

Most people are not comfortable with knowing what the future is. They feel it takes away the adventure of living, so they will live in a miserable state of not-know, thinking that's creating the adventure of living. Actually, knowing is the greatest adventure there is. You know it's going to happen, you just have no idea how it's going to happen. And finding out how it shows up is way more fun than not knowing that it will show up.

Are you looking at something greater than what you currently have? Or are you looking at what you currently have as the best you can get? If you look to the present as the best you're going to get, you're trying to make yourself satisfied with no more than you currently have. Being satisfied with no more than what you currently have doesn't give you a place to create and generate the *more* that is the innate response of an infinite being.

Stop trying to solidify your future.

Create your future. You do that with choice.

You Have to Create Today to Have What
You Want Tomorrow

I highly recommend Steve and Chutisa's Bowman's book, *Living from the Edge of Possibility*. It's about how to create your life as well as your business. In it, they talk about Steve Jobs, whose point of view was that even if he had spent millions trying to develop something, when a better idea came along, he'd drop the millions he had spent and develop the new idea. He was willing to destroy and uncreate everything that was yesterday, so he was constantly on a creative edge in the present.

Most people are trying to be on the cutting edge of things, but being on the cutting edge means you're always ready to be sliced and diced. Being on the creative edge means you're always in a mode of question, choice, possibility, and contribution. That's the place you need to live from. Being on the creative edge means you're not going to stop yourself because you created something. You continue to create.

I had a friend once who used to make pottery. He worked with the thick, dense clay potters used in the 1970s, and he would make thin, delicate pieces that felt like porcelain. He was a big, hulking guy with massive hands, arms, and shoulders, and he would use his strength to create delicate, fragile pots. He'd fire them, take them out of the kiln, and say, "Oh, this thing is cracked," and he'd throw it on the ground and shatter it into a million pieces.

I'd say, "No, please don't do that! Let me buy it!"

He'd say, "No, it's not good enough." He was willing to throw away what he saw as not good enough rather than putting out something that was less than what he knew was possible.

How about the rest of us? Are we doing that in our lives? Are we throwing away what isn't possible? Are we holding onto what hasn't worked as though some day, it might be valuable? Get rid of what doesn't work and then you can create.

This is what you need to do as well in your business, your life, and your relationship. Destroy and uncreate everything that was yesterday so you can be on the creative edge of things today. Destroying and uncreating yesterday undoes the solidity of your future and makes it spacious. It's the pragmatic thing to do if you wish to go beyond something that doesn't work and onto something that *will* work.

What does work is creating today. You have to create today in order to have what you want tomorrow. If you don't institute things today, if you don't generate and create today, when you get to the future, you're not going to have what you'd like to have.

I know people who work really hard to get their rent together, then once they get it, they think, "Whew, that's done!" and they go back to being sedentary. They wait until the next emergency comes along. Then, once again, they work like crazy to take care of the rent or the car repair bill or whatever it is. Many people live with this start-and-stall system. It's "Hurry up and get it done so you can have it handled—and then don't do anything."

I don't function that way. I ask, "What do I need to handle today?" I never reach the conclusion that I have anything handled forever. It's never done for the future, because everything you create today should be something that contributes to your future. It's not something that is "finished" or "done." Does energy ever complete? No. It can change, it can alter—but it can't complete. So, why do we assume that we are not like energy—something that's never really completed?

Don't ask, "What do I need to complete today?" Create your future by asking:

- What else is possible today?

- What else do I have to do today?

- What else can be created beyond this?

More than one option may come up when you ask these questions. Some people may try to apply the light/heavy tool* to their choices, to see what feels light or heavy and choose on the basis of that. I don't look from there. I look from the viewpoint:

- Which one of these choices is going to create the life I'd like to have in five years? If I get no clear answer, I ask:

- Is there a way to get both of these options to work together?

- Is there another option I haven't considered?

When I ask, "Is there some other option I haven't considered?" clarity becomes part of the construct of the future I'm trying to create.

Other questions you can use whenever you lack clarity are:

- Is this choice going to be better than that one?

- If I choose this, what will my life be like in five years?

- If I don't choose this, what will my life be like in five years?

If one option feels slightly better than the other, but the other one doesn't feel bad, ask:

- What are the other options I haven't considered?

- What if we used both of these at different times?

- What if we did different events with different approaches?

These questions will give you a sense that there is always a different possibility so you can create today to have what you want tomorrow.

---

* The light/heavy tool is an Access Consciousness® tool based on the fact that what's true for you will always make you feel lighter.

So, What Creates the Future?

Your choice creates the future. You make a choice today and the future gets created by that choice. Each choice creates a cobweb of possibilities. Every time you choose something, at least ten different possibilities open up. From those possibilities, you have a minimum of ten choices. If you choose again, another ten possibilities open up. Each choice slowly but surely leads you to the future you are capable of being.

You may think that processing creates your future. It doesn't. Processing erases your past, but it does not create your future. Your choice creates your future. You've got to choose, choose, choose before you lose, lose, lose.

If you want the Kingdom of True Choice, ask, "What is this choice going to create?" Earlier I talked about this in terms of relationship. I suggested you ask, "If I choose this person, what will this relationship be like in six months? Nine months? A year? Two years?" I didn't ask you to go further than two years because most people can't sustain a relationship for longer than two years. Do you know why? Because when they think about their relationship more than two years into the future, they try to solidify the future. They try to fill in the space with what they think a relationship that goes longer than two years would or should be like. They try to fill it in with something that's solid enough to match what their past and their present have been.

The Kingdom of True Choice is recognizing that the choices you make today create the future. When you attempt to define the future or to contract or solidify your choices, you limit what's possible. The choices you made in past lives are affecting you and probably limiting you today. Why? Because you solidified those choices as the right or wrong choice. You didn't ask, "How is this choice creating a future that's going to work for me?" When you do "right" or "wrong," you destroy the possibility of a future that has expansiveness and possibility as its primary motivating factor.

You must be in communion not just with the past and present, but with the future as well, because the future is part of the universe. You have to be willing to see how your energies are creating your future, because every choice creates.

Creation is part of oneness. If we were actually willing to be communion with all things, then your creation would be as my creation, and I could be a contribution to your creation.

The one thing most people are not comfortable with is total choice. They try to live in this reality rather than creating their reality. To live in this reality only requires you to have three choices: Right or wrong, good or bad, positive or negative. You think, "I've made my choice. Why would I need any other choice?" And you're not willing to discard your choice once you've chosen it, even if it's not working for you. None of this has to do with the Kingdom of True Choice.

When you are truly creating from future, you create multiple choices instead of one. Do you like just one flower at a time or do you like bouquets of many different flowers? Why would you make just one choice when you can make many? What if choice is a bouquet you can have the fragrance of? You can throw it away in a heartbeat, rearrange it, or do anything you desire with it. You can have the bouquet of choice, which allows you to change it at any time, throw away the dead blossoms, and choose again.

Choice means you create other choices. We keep trying to choose one thing, thinking that one thing is going to be the thing that gives us the future we want to have. It's no longer about being aware of what's possible; it's about the future we have decided we desire.

I have a friend who was intent on preparing for a universe of success for now and all time. She had created a concept of what her future was going to be and she was not willing to destroy and uncreate that concept. She thought she had to choose one thing and stick with it until it was dead. Is this something you do as well? Do you say things like "The only choice I have is taking this class" or "The only choice I have is doing something drastic to solve my problem"? It's as if you're asking, "How sad and unhappy can I be and still survive?" You choose based on your back door, which is always rooted in the idea that there is going to be a lack in your life. You think playing with your back door is more entertaining than choosing something different. You have misidentified that as amusement. You think lack of choice is more entertaining than full choice, so you keep yourself amused by falling into your future by accident.

What destruction of future are you choosing with the lack of choice you misidentify as amusing? Everything that is times a godzillion, will you destroy and uncreate it all? Right and wrong, good and bad, POC and POD, all 9, shorts, boys, and beyonds.

When you have full choice, nothing matters. Nothing is important. Nothing is significant. Everything is just choice. If you have total choice at all times, are you going to make your limitations amusing to you? No. You've got to get that you have been amused by your limitations for a long time, but that party is over now. You now know you have the Kingdom of True Choice.

What future are you capable of,

that you don't even know you're capable of?

Scan for more information

◊

BEING PRESENT IN EVERY MOMENT
OF YOUR LIFE

What if the target of your life was to have fun, to be present,

and to experience every moment to the fullest?

Would that be better than getting to the end of your life and knowing

you've accomplished everything you were supposed to accomplish

according to someone else's point of view?

The Meditation Walk

For a long time, I have noticed that most people are not comfortable with themselves. They feel like they need to do something rather than simply *be*.

You have created your whole life according to other people's points of view, their needs, their wants, and their desires. You don't get that it's easier for you to be aware of what other people want, require, or desire because you've never chosen what you need, want, and desire. You haven't been taught to be present with you, as you. Instead you have been told that if you *do* enough, everything will work out. To me, not being totally present as me, with me, all the time, seems insane. But that's not what we're taught in this reality. Have you noticed that? We're taught to move from point A to point B as quickly as possible.

I asked how I could get people to the point where they could begin to recognize that being comfortable with themselves is not about having to *do*; it's about the willingness to *be*. The meditation walk came up as a way to present them with another option. The idea of this walk is to experience being present in the space you are in. It is about you being present with you—and everything else around you.

I'd like to invite you to do the meditation walk now. Here is how it is done:

- You have to take one hour to walk 100 feet (thirty meters).

- You are not allowed to talk to anybody.

- You're not allowed to look at anybody.

- You have to be present in every moment throughout the entire hour.

You'll have to select a place where you can do this. Preferably, this would be a place where there are no other people around, except perhaps others who are doing the walk as well.

I invite you to be present with you in a way you have never been, which means you have to pay attention to you, to every movement of your body, and to everything that's going on in and around you. You'll see the insects on the ground, you'll hear things in the air, you'll be aware of all kinds of stuff. You are not allowed to talk to anybody. You are not allowed to get together with anybody. You are not allowed to think that anybody is cuter than you are.

You have to take an hour to go 100 feet. You have to be in total presence to manage not to go farther than 100 feet in an hour. You are able to move, but you don't have to move. You have choice.

We often do the meditation walk at Access Consciousness® events, and it's interesting to observe the people who are totally present and comfortable with themselves. They move, but they don't feel like they have to move. They enjoy themselves.

Others get uncomfortable. They feel they have to move when they sense the intensity of their presence. I watched one man who continuously needed to move. After the walk, I asked him, "Do you have a sense that this is what you have to do in your life as well?"

He said, "Oh yeah."

I said, "You've got to get to the point where you don't need to move and you have an awareness of when and how and what to move. It's 'I am making a choice to move—or not.' You'll recognize, 'I don't have to lie still in order to have me, and I don't have to move to have me. I can be me, no matter what the circumstance is.'"

The choice you make to move creates a change in all reality, not just yours. Your movement creates a change in everything around you.

When you are totally present with your body, you feel the muscles and the sinews, the heartbeat, the blood flow, and the energy flows. You're aware with your kinesthetic awareness, not just with your eyes and ears and your sense of touch, smell, and taste.

You can live your life like this, with this kind of intensity, presence, and awareness of the space of you—the space you are being and in which you are doing what you are doing.

So, at this point, please do the meditation walk.

- Take one hour to walk 100 feet (thirty meters), being present with you, your body, and everything around you.

- Do not talk to anybody.

- Do not look at anybody.

- Just be present.

What Did You Do on the Meditation Walk

Did you make a decision when you first started to do it?

Did you come to conclusions, decisions, and judgments about how it was going to be?

Did you try to make the exercise right—or to make it wrong?

Did you ask, "Why is he telling me to do this?"

Did you say, "I don't want to do this"?

That's the way you live your life. Is that real choice? No. Choice begins the moment you're willing to create. It doesn't begin with the decisions you make.

Or did you ask, "What's available here that I haven't considered?"

That's the way I live my life. I never know what's going to show up day by day. Do I know what the future is going to bring? Yes, I know the future is going to be greater than yesterday. I know the future is going to be something that's valuable to me because I'm doing everything I can today to create a future that's more expansive than the one that currently exists. That's called living.

I never ask, "Will my life be better tomorrow? Will I have more money tomorrow?" That is not the place I function from. I ask, "What choices can I make today that will create a better reality than what currently exists?"

For me, every single moment of every single day is as intense as that one-hour walk you just took. Are you willing to have your life be that intense?

What Did You Do on the Walk?

The things you did on the walk are the ways you live your life. Those things are your solutions to being present.

Did you run to the edge of the 100 feet and then sit there? Your solution to being present is to go quickly to what you've decided you want to accomplish and then move around in order to prove you've gotten there.

Were you present with your body in the way you stood, the way you walked, and the way you moved? Most people either stand outside their body and fall into it or they stand behind it and shove it. Very few people walk in their body. You actually have to be present with your body and walk in your body when you do the meditation walk.

Did you become aware of a lot of things that you tried not to pay attention to? Why have you chosen to cut off your awareness? Because everybody else does? Or because that is the only way you could stand the intensity of your awareness? Would you like to give that up? Would you like to stand in the intensity and joy of your awareness?

Did you have a hard time just being present? It's okay if you did, because you have that awareness, and now you can change it.

Whatever you got out of the walk is not about the rightness or wrongness of what you got. It's about seeing that what you got gives you an indication of how you're living your life. Once you see the way you're living, you get to ask, "Is this the way I want to live— or do I want more? Is there something else that would be greater for me that I haven't chosen?"

I am hoping you got a sense of "I'll experience what I am experiencing as I get to where I'm getting. I'll be aware of everything I am aware of as I get to where I get to." Not "I have to get there," but "What else is possible?"

When you are present as you, when you are enjoying your body, when you're being you, you cannot help but be joyful. When you are more present, you are more joyful. When you're willing to be with everything the world is willing to give you, what you can have in your life is much greater than you ever considered.

Have you been unwilling to commit to

your true level of awareness?

Every Conscious Element on This Earth Desires to Support You

The trees are supporting you, the plants, the animals, the flowers, the bees, the insects, and everything around you wants to support your consciousness. Every conscious element on this Earth desires to support you. Are you willing to receive it? Or do you try to cut that out of your awareness?

You keep thinking you're all alone and that nobody has your back. You know what? The birds have your back and every molecule of the soil has your back. The Earth has your back. The Earth wants to support you. The Earth wants you to be as great as you are. Why are you not choosing that?

Everything in the universe, every molecule in the universe, is in communion with you. Everything will support you if you are willing to receive that support. But you keep acting as if nothing supports you and nothing wants to contribute to you. You keep acting as if you're all alone and no one is for you.

Why won't you receive this support? It's your judgment. You say, "Well, this city is blah-blah-blah." You won't receive what the city has to give you. You don't ask the question, "How does the city contribute to me?" I can get as much from the concrete as I get from the grass in a park. I can get as much from metal as I get from a flower. I have no judgment of the metal. I have no judgment of the flower. I am willing to recognize every molecule of everything in the world is a consciousness that will contribute to me if I'm willing to receive it.

For me, being in the city is no different from being in the forest. Each is an expansiveness that is available to me—if I'm willing to be it. You've got to be willing to be that expansiveness. Then you can have it at any time. Otherwise, you're always going to have to see the separation of you from everything else. The thing is, it's a separation that doesn't actually exist. It's a creation. You just have to make the choice.

The Earth wants to care for you. It wants to gift to you all the time. Every plant, every animal wants to give to you. I have people who work with my horses, who get how much the horses want to contribute. They have created miracles with these horses because they see that the horse wants to contribute. The horses are there and they are doing everything they can and they truly desire to contribute to us. But so does every other molecule in the entire universe.

You aren't receiving that for what reason? Why do you think that receiving is somebody giving you money? Why do you think receiving is somebody giving you validation? Why do you think at all?

All have to do is choose to be conscious,

and the universe will support you.

It's your choice.

I once lived in a house where there was a little flower pot by the door. Every year birds would come, build a nest there, and raise their babies. How many birds build a nest by a door where people go in and out a lot? They usually don't. But obviously there was a sense of peace, presence, and contribution that was going to protect them. That's what they chose. It was so fun to watch the baby birds doing their thing, and the parents whipping in and feeding them.

We'd go out the door and say, "How are you doing, guys?" And the baby birds would go, "Tweet, tweet, tweet." The parents would come down and feed the babies while we were standing in the doorway. Birds do that only when you're being the energy that allows them to recognize that you are not a threat; you are a contribution. Please understand: There's so much available to you. All you've got to do is choose it.

Have you been cutting off your awareness of all the consciousness that wants to support you, to be there for you, and to make your life the joy that it is for you?

What haven't you chosen that you could choose,

that if you would choose it,

would create the reality you would like to have?

Scan for more information

*　*　*

This book has been designed to create a reality that is not linear or dimensional; it has been designed to create a spherical reality, because from a sphere, everything is available and there is only choice, which creates where you are in the sphere of things.

My hope is that you've begun to get an idea of what your life could be like in a spherical reality. A sphere never contracts. It is an ever-growing, ever-expanding universe. That is what your universe can be. If you are the sphere of reality, you become a sphere of influence on the entire world and everybody around you. What would it be like if you were the spherical contribution to a spherical reality that has never existed before? Choose!

◊

THE CLEARING STATEMENT

The Clearing Statement

In Access Consciousness®, there is a clearing process we use to destroy and uncreate blockages and limitations, which are really just stuck energy. Once we become aware of an energy that we wish to clear, we simply say the clearing statement. It may seem like the clearing statement is about the words (which are expressed in short-speak) but really, it is the energy of the clearing statement that changes things, not the words.

The words of the clearing statement are: Right and wrong, good and bad, POD and POC, all 9, shorts, boys and beyonds. Here's a brief description of what they mean:

Right and wrong, good and bad is shorthand for: What's right, good, perfect and correct about this? What's wrong, mean, vicious, terrible, bad, and awful about this? The short version of these questions is: What's right and wrong, good and bad?

POD and POC

POC stands for the **P**oint **o**f **C**reation of the thoughts, feelings and emotions immediately preceding your decision to lock the energy in place. POD stands for the **P**oint **o**f **D**estruction of the thoughts, feelings and emotions immediately preceding any decisions to lock that item in place and all the ways you have been destroying yourself in order to keep it in existence.

POD and POC is also an abbreviated way of saying "destroy and uncreate."

When you "POD and POC" something, it is like pulling the bottom card out of a house of cards. The whole thing falls down.

All 9 stands for the nine different ways you have created this item as a limitation in your life. They are the layers of thoughts, feelings, emotions and points of view that create the limitation as solid and real.

Shorts is the short version of a much longer series of questions that include: What's meaningful about this? What's meaningless about this? What's the punishment for this? What's the reward for this?

Boys stands for energetic structures called nucleated spheres. There are thirty-two different kinds of these spheres, which are collectively called "the boys." A nucleated sphere looks like the bubbles created when you blow in one of those kids' bubble pipes that has multiple chambers. It creates a huge mass of bubbles, and when you pop one bubble, the other bubbles fill in the space.

Have you ever tried to peel the layers of an onion when you were trying to get to the core of an issue, but you could never get there? That's because it wasn't an onion; it was a nucleated sphere.

Beyonds are feelings or sensations you get that stop your heart, stop your breath, or stop your willingness to look at possibilities. Beyonds are what occur when you are in shock. The beyonds include everything that is beyond belief, reality, imagination, conception, perception, rationalization, forgiveness as well as all the other beyonds. They are usually feelings and sensations, rarely emotions, and never thoughts.

◊

THE GOLDEN PLANET

The First Three Chapters of a Novel

by Gary M. Douglas

Introduction

Welcome to the Golden Planet. It doesn't exist anymore, but it still drives us all to know that more is possible than what we experience and that the thread of unknown magic must exist.

This story occurred or was created about four trillion years ago. You don't believe in past lives? Neither did I, but I do now. The memory or story or reality of the planet has seeped into existence and downloaded its parts into my life over the last thirty years, yet I don't know what to say or do about it. That's why I am writing this book.

For years I tried to understand what was weird about this reality and this world, and there was a niggling sense at the back of my mind or consciousness or sub-consciousness that everything should be easier. More should be possible. I always felt sort of cheated by the kind of effort it seemed to take to create or do anything. As a child, I just knew that life didn't have to be so very hard.

The Golden Planet has given me an awareness of what I knew as a child ought to be possible. The story that follows may help you to realize that there is a reason for the dreams and feelings of possibilities that never become realities and why and how and where they might actually exist. And maybe we can get there yet.

Chapter 1

His name is Gareth.

He is Head of the College of Expanded Awareness and Consciousness, one of the highest honors on the planet, for here on Oramas, awareness is the job of every citizen. Each of us is a part of the whole, as all things are interrelated and all things belong to the oneness that we are, and each of us is also of necessity the source for the creation of what is and what will be.

As Gareth looks over the balustrade towards the green grass below, he watches the dirt and sand play around the bottom of the golden tree that shakes and sways as though caught in the wind. Tiny flakes of gold filter to the ground as Dalin, his ward, swings his hands in the air, orchestrating the currents of dust and dirt and guiding them to become what his heart desires. The golden swirls of dust and the sweet breezes of glittering gift combine in the dance of consciousness that all molecular structure is and they take the beautiful form of freedom and joy that is Dalin's vision of the house he would like to have. It is quite amazing to see this small body with the big being doing such advanced work at such an early point in the growth of his body. On Oramas, most bodies are created from the genetic material of three donors, but this being has chosen the genetic material of five donors to create the body he desires. Perhaps that is part of the explanation of what makes him so advanced; of course, there are some secret reasons as well.

As Gareth puts these thoughts forward, the child-being looks up and smiles, and the amusement in the thoughts that return to Gareth are the beginning of a delight that reaches every sensorial element of his body. As he bursts into laughter, the birds begin to sing with intensity to match his and the plants lean toward the joy that feeds their souls as much as his. Gareth knows that this being is the one who will carry the secrets of the Golden Planet until the awakening. It will only take four trillion years by the standards of time of the visitors who will impel the concept of time upon the realities of those who live on Oramas.

As he ponders all that is the awareness of the future that he wishes would not be, there is a knock at the door. So deep in thought and contemplation was he that he did not sense her coming. "Enter, please" is the thought he sends to her, for speech is not yet part of the need or desire on Oramas.

Kalisondra enters, her imperious demeanor shielding thoughts that only Gareth can access. His capacity to access what she desires to hide tells him that she has come for purposes of her own, not as part of her job. He recognizes that her desire to hide what needs to be hidden in order to create lies and subterfuge will equal difficulties and problems where there should be none. She moves her bulk across the floor with a smoothness and grace that few of her size can achieve, and the effort leaves a line of sweat trickling down the side of her face. The molecular structure of her body screams with the contraction of space that is required to keep her secret and pretend that nothing is going on in her head. She seats herself in the golden chair that is reserved for truly special guests, and her automatic choice tells something of what is going on in her mind.

Gareth lowers the shields that are the normal space in which he can create and know more, and he sends the question to her, "What is it you need of me today?" Kalisondra has never realized that by adding "today" to the missives he sends, Gareth eliminates others' capacity to see the future that is so obvious to him, and their lack of knowing gives him access to what they desire to keep secret, because today's secret is tomorrow's lie.

Kalisondra blinks as she senses the search of her universe, which is normal for all on Oramas, yet she has always tried to shield this space from others to protect what she has ascertained to be the creation of personal space, a growing concept of faith upon the planet. "So odd," thinks Gareth, "that personal space would be valuable when total awareness gives access to all the energy, space, and consciousness that one could ever desire."

This concept of personal space began when Kalisondra came up with the idea of the College of Judges, to which she was instantly elected by her followers. The purpose of the college was to judge who could and could not molecularly actualize their vision in any one space. It had never been necessary before the citizenship voted to have personal space as a conceptual reality they would serve and play with. As a result of personal space, people accepted the idea that there was a need to determine and judge what was most appropriate for any space or creation.

Gareth allowed Kalisondra to know his lack of approval in the concept of judgment being a necessity to create and he let her read his lack of resentment and the expansiveness that oneness gave as a remarkable sense of the choice that every molecule has to be. She did not want him to see the irritation in her world that the gift of choice the universe gives is information about the future.

It was odd to Gareth, with the whole universe willing to support them and gift all that they asked, that this creation of self as a female structure of size and intensity required the allegiance of followers to have no inkling of the power that is gifted to each who chooses consciousness. Apparently that was not a gift that Kalisondra desired at all.

She begins to deliver in giant gulps of information all that is planned by her and her followers, and Gareth receives the awareness of those who are on her team and not yet on the planet and who will soon arrive to start the seduction that she has already succumbed to: the visitors becoming part of the reality of Oramas, changing everything that has ever been, starting a road to a future that would make all less than what they would be or could be, and requiring those who understood what true consciousness offered to suffer in order to make consciousness a construct for the creation of a new universe, far away in time and space.

The solidification of what Kalisondra had decided was the way things had to be began to be, and it struck Gareth that great separation was required to make what was part of being become the source for limitation and painful intrusion upon another.

It becomes obvious to Gareth that what is being impelled at him is creating a construct that is not part of his reality but is being given to Kalisondra and her followers by the visitors who are coming to Oramas. At that moment, a new concept falls into existence for him. Control. He senses it as the energy that is required to conceptually hold all that is possible away from others, so they must turn to Kalisondra and the visitors for the awareness that is part of being, their own awareness thus ceasing to exist so the new leaders can incorporate followers into their reality and eliminate the choices that create all possibilities and everything that would take them to functioning within the oneness in which all is included and judgement has no value. Gareth senses this concept, as he does so many other things, as the twisting of what *is* into that which *isn't*, as though that is the way to create value.

With that, another concept is impelled into his awareness, the idea of value and the hierarchy of value. It is something that has long escaped his understanding. Suddenly he receives what the visitors have made so real to Kalisondra, and which he had not been able to fathom: that the construct of society as a valuable component of control and purpose (another foreign concept) gives rise to diminishment of communion with all molecular structures, which form as one chooses into whatever one asks and instead becomes a need for the structures of creation as incremental separations of the molecules into form that only the leaders have access to and from.

Kalisondra, the density of her body increasing as she explodes her desire for that which from her reckoning, will make her the most powerful person on the planet, shines with the perspiration that is so rare on Oramas that few ever experience it. Her mind is a jumble of images and ideas that are not the substance of this place, but obviously belong to the visitors who are coming soon.

"When are you new friends coming?" Gareth thinks at her. Her energy warps into a hyperdrive of shutdown to hide what has been exposed, and Gareth receives the not-so-satisfactory screaming of the molecular structures around him as they are gathered to the storm of secrecy that has been Kalisondra's best and most useful weapon to overwhelm others. But still, the intensity of the hidden increases the magnitude of the awareness that these beings will be here within the seventh day.

Chapter 2

They came.

Gareth sensed them, much as he sensed the lightning storms that created rain and changed the atmosphere of the planet, a cleansing energy that soothed the ground and blessed the creatures. Energy that invigorated all life in the gift and contribution to changing what had become stagnant from the insufficiency of change that is the primary consciousness of all molecular structures. This energy would be neither cleansing nor life giving, but it had the similar charge of electrical pulse that would change or annihilate.

He could sense their presence even before they became visible. Kalisondra's personal joy and exuberance raced before them as her sense of personal power, certain to be finally attained, exuded from the entirety of her body. Its electrical charge was much like the lightning, in that it too was destined to change molecular activation.

Two of them came to him first with Kalisondra, and without his invitation, she directed them to the golden seats of honor. The energy that exuded from them was tormenting to Gareth. He searched their energy fields and could sense a strange need as a concept now brought to substance. He had never known need himself, and experiencing that strange and totally uncomfortable reality, he began to suspect that they had been in contact with Kalisondra for many seasons.

With that recognition, came a new concept they called time. Time, how odd when all things are possible and all molecules communicate with one. Time has no reality, yet the strangers saw value in it and exuded it as the construct which justified everything as a series of dependences. He staggered from his awareness of the sacrifices that all on Oramas would make to this thing called time.

For many seasons, even before Dalin chose his genetic donors, Gareth had sensed a strange prickling at the back of his head. Now it all came together with a host of other moments to give the clarity, the gift of total awareness.

So strange that beings would seek what these seem to seek. Gareth becomes aware of the odd prickling again and realizes he is being probed. They are using some odd-looking jewel to accomplish what the children of Oramas do with ease. The probing is obviously looking for some kind of resistance, yet Gareth has none. The probing ceases and major elements of coarseness appear in their energy field. He senses the strange thing that only Kalisondra and her followers have ever emanated. A new concept descends into his universe. It is called confusion.

The visitors, now aware, or so they think, and yet another concept descends into Gareth's awareness. That beings would use *thought* instead of *knowing* is so strange that for a moment, he lacks the strength to follow how odd and limited the energy is which creates thought. Now he understands Kalisondra and the bulk that has become her physical actualization. One must *think* in order to diminish knowing, and that seals all contractions into the creation of physical reality.

Chapter 3

Days have passed and the visitors, using their technology, have begun their seduction of those on Oramas, something that has never existed on Oramas because total communion with the molecules around one allows one to envision and actualize in an instant anything one wishes. There is no destruction necessary for creation, only the need to request change. When one asks, the molecules adjust themselves to create the change that has been requested. That is the law of the universe, "As you ask, so shall you receive."

The visitors are introducing the population to something they call the vibrational virtual realities of different planets and locations that exist in what they call the known Galaxy. It is funny to Gareth and the others who practice the art of knowing that there cannot be an awareness of that which has already been discovered and seen and that if one has not seen it, it doesn't exist. For the College of Expanded Awareness and Consciousness, knowing that which has not yet been observed does not eliminate that which can be perceived, and with that perception, one is able to choose how it can actualize and be.

Apparently, for the visitors this is a foreign idea; it is not of any use to them in what they seek, but what they seek has not been revealed, because they hide it with the contraction that has created the bulk of Kalisondra as well as the machinery that seems so magnificent to so many on Oramas, mostly because none of it has ever been needed or desired.

About the Author

Gary M. Douglas

Best-selling author, international speaker and a sought-after facilitator, Gary Douglas is known for his intensity of awareness and his incredible capacity to facilitate people to *"know what they know."* He chooses to embody consciousness in everything that he does which inspires others to choose to become more conscious as a result.

Gary came with an exceptional level of awareness into the Midwest middle class "white bread" family and lived the "Leave it to Beaver" childhood. He has a very different view on life and realized that he was so different from most of the people he knew when he was only six years old. He became aware of this difference by watching people create their lives and seeing that none of it was about the joy and the possibilities—it was always about the wrongness of everything. Gary knew there had to be more than this reality was offering since there was nothing about it that was magical, joyful or expansive. So, he began seeking deeper awareness to life's mysteries at an early age. Along the way he uncovered a new way forward- one that would create change in the world and in people's lives. He discovered that magic is all around us; it's something we create—its consciousness. He recognized that the capacity to be more aware and more conscious was every person's gift if they were willing to choose it.

Over time what he recognised as the gift he was, was his intensity of awareness and his capacity to invite people to consciousness and to recognise that everything is possible and nothing is impossible. His gift is his ability to look at life, the universe and the consciousness that we all are, as well as the possibilities that are an intrinsic part of it from a space that no one else has ever chosen.

Empowering people to see different possibilities

Gary has become an internationally recognized thought leader in transforming lives and creating different choices—willing to empower people to see different possibilities and to recognize what is truly possible for them. Gary is acknowledged worldwide for his unique perspectives on personal transformation that is unlike anything else in the world. He is not aligned with any particular religion or tradition. Through his writing and workshops, he gifts processes and tools that bring within reach the ease, joy and glory of life, and the magic of happiness that expand into more awareness, joy and abundance. His simple yet profound teachings have already facilitated countless people throughout the world to 'know what they know' and to realize what they can choose that they never realised they could choose.

At the core of his teachings
lies the transformation of consciousness

After recognising that greater consciousness in people can change the direction of their lives and the future of the planet, the creation and expansion of Access Consciousness® by Gary has been primarily driven by a single question, "What can I do to help the world?"

He continues to inspire others, inviting the awareness of a different possibility across the world and making an immense contribution to the planet. He facilitates people to know that they are the source for creating the change they desire and creating a life that goes beyond the limitations of what the rest of the world thinks is important. He sees this as an essential aspect to creating a future that has greater possibilities in it for everyone as well as the planet. This is a priority not only for personal happiness but also for the ending of violent conflict endemic on our planet and creating a different world. If enough people choose to be more aware and more conscious, they will start to see the possibilities of what they have available to them and change what is occurring here on planet earth.

Author

He is the author of the bestselling novel *The Place*. The book is about people knowing that all things are possible, and choice is the source of creation. Gary is also the co-author of a variety of books on the subjects of money, relationships, magic and animals with internationally renowned Energy Transformation virtuoso Dr. Dain Heer.

Inspiring people worldwide

Gary pioneered a set of transformational life changing tools and processes known as Access Consciousness® over 20 years ago. These leading edge tools have transformed the lives of thousands of people all over the world. His work has spread to 47 countries, with 2,000 trained facilitators worldwide. Simple but so effective, the tools facilitate people of all ages and backgrounds to help remove limitations holding them back from a full life.

Access Consciousness® Core Classes

If you liked what you read in this book and are interested in attending Access seminars, workshops or classes, then for a very different point of view, read-on and sample a taste of what is available. These are the core classes in Access Consciousness®.

Access Bars™

Facilitated by Certified Access Bars Facilitators worldwide

The first class in Access Consciousness® is The Bars. Did you know there are 32 points on your head, which when gently touched, effortlessly and easily release the thoughts, ideas, beliefs, emotions and considerations you have stored in any lifetime?

Is your life not yet what you would like it to be? You could have everything you desire (and then some!) if you were willing to receive more and do a little less! Receiving or learning The Bars will allow this—and so much more—to show up for you!

The Bars class is a prerequisite for all Access Consciousness® Core Classes, as it allows your body to process and receive with ease all the changes you are choosing.

Duration: 1 day

Access Foundation

Facilitated by Certified Access Facilitators worldwide

After the Access Bars, this two-day class is about giving you the space to look at your life as a different possibility.

Unlock your limitations about embodiment, finances, success, relationships, family, YOU and your capacities, and much more!

Step into greater possibilities for having everything you truly desire in life as you learn tools and questions to change anything that's not working for you. You also learn a hands-on body process called Cellular Memory that works wonders on scars and pains in the body! If you could change anything in your life, what would it be?

Prerequisite: Access Bars
Duration: 2 days

Access Level 1

Facilitated by Certified Access Facilitators worldwide

After Access Foundation, Level 1 is a two-day class that shows you how to be more conscious in every area of your life and gives you practical tools that allow you to continue expanding this in your day-to-day! Create a phenomenal life filled with magic, joy and ease and clear your limitations about what is truly available for you.

Discover the 5 Elements of Intimacy, create energy flows, start laughing and celebrating living and practice a hands-on body process that has created miraculous results all over the world!

Prerequisite: Access Foundation
Duration: 2 days

Access Levels 2 & 3

Facilitated Exclusively by Gary Douglas (Founder of Access Consciousness®) and Dr. Dain Heer

Having completed Level 1 and opened up to more awareness of you, you start to have more choice in life and become aware of what choice truly is. This four-day class covers a huge range of areas, including the joy of business, living life for the fun of it, no fear, courage and leadership, changing the molecular structure of things, creating your body and your sexual reality, and how to stop holding on to what you want to get rid of! Is it time to start receiving the change you've been asking for?

Prerequisites: Access Bars, Foundation and Level 1
Duration: 4 days (2 days for Level 2 & 2 days for Level 3)

Access Body Class

Facilitated by Access Body Class Facilitators worldwide

During this three-day class you will learn verbal processes and hands-on bodywork that unlock the tension, resistance, and dis-ease of the body. Do you have a talent and ability to work with bodies that you haven't yet unlocked? Are you a body worker (massage therapist, chiropractor, medical doctor, nurse) looking for a way to enhance the healing you can do for your clients? Come play with us and begin to explore how to communicate and relate to bodies, including yours, in a whole new way.

Prerequisite: Access Bars
Duration: 3 days

Advanced Access Body Class with Gary Douglas

This class offers a unique set of new body processes that give your body the possibility of going beyond the limitations of this reality. What if you could undo the limitations locked into your body that create an alteration of the way it functions? What if your body could become far more efficient? What if you and your body didn't have to function the way everyone in this reality believes they have to?

What if food, supplements and exercise have almost nothing to do with how your body truly functions? What if you could have ease, joy and communion with your body far beyond what is considered possible right now? Would you be willing to explore the possibilities?

Prerequisites: Access Bars, Foundation, Levels 1, 2 & 3 &
the 3-day Access Body Class two times
Duration: 3 days

3-Day Energetic Synthesis of Being Class with Dr. Dain Heer

This class is your invitation to come and play with the universe.

In this class, Dain works on one person in front of the group—and on everyone in the room—at the same time. During this time, your being, your body and the earth are invited to energetically synthesize in a way that creates a more conscious life and a more conscious planet.

You will discover that you can become a gift to the planet by being the energies of caring, nurturing, honoring, allowance and gratitude. By being these energies, by being you, you change everything; the planet, your life and everyone you come into contact with. What else is possible then?

Open doors to change, to awareness, and to a universe of oneness and consciousness.

Prerequisites: Access Bars, Foundation & Levels 1, 2 & 3
Duration: 3 days

Energetic Synthesis of Being – The Beginning
with Dr. Dain Heer

During this beginning class, Dain will give participants a taste of what is possible in the three-day Energetic Synthesis of Being intensive.

3½ Day Being You, Changing the World Class
with Dr. Dain Heer

There is only one thing you were born to do. You were born to be YOU. Not the "you" your partner, your society or your parents want you to be. It isn't about being successful or doing anything better. It is about being YOU!

What if you, being you, is all it takes to change everything: your life, everyone around you and the world?

This class presents the possibility of implementing deeply penetrating tools to effect profound change in your life. It's easy to do—all that is required of you is a willingness to ask for and choose to be the truth of you.

Together with the group, you'll explore the very energies of living. You'll get tangible, practical and transformative tools that will allow you to start finding out what is true for you and access your knowing of who you truly BE.

Duration: 3½ days

Being You, Changing the World – The Beginning
with Dr. Dain Heer

This one-evening class, which is open to everyone, will give you a taste of what else is possible in your life. It is also the beginning of the 3½ Day Being You, Changing the World Class.

Access Consciousness® 7-Day Events

Are you an adventurer and a seeker of ever-greater possibilities? Are you willing to consider questions you've never asked before? And are you ready to receive more change than you can imagine? If so, the 7-day event just might be for you!

These invitation-only, freeform classes are held twice a year in beautiful locations around the world by Access Consciousness founder, Gary Douglas. To be invited, you must have attended at least one Level 2 & 3 class in person.

There is no other class or event like this offered anywhere in the world. It is a unique and life-changing experience.

Prerequisites: Level 2 and 3
Duration: 7 days

Other Access Consciousness® Books

Being You, Changing the World
By Dr. Dain Heer

Have you always known that something COMPLETELY DIFFERENT is possible? What if you had a handbook for infinite possibilities and dynamic change to guide you? With tools and processes that actually worked and invited you to a completely different way of being? For you? And the world?

The Ten Keys to Total Freedom
By Gary M. Douglas & Dr. Dain Heer

The Ten Keys to Total Freedom are a way of living that will help you expand your capacity for consciousness so that you can have greater awareness about yourself, your life, this reality and beyond. With greater awareness you can begin creating the life you've always known was possible but haven't yet achieved. If you will actually do and be these things, you will get free in every aspect of your life.

Embodiment:
The Manual You Should Have Been Given
When You Were Born
By Dr. Dain Heer

The information you should have been given at birth, about bodies, about being you and what is truly possible if you choose it... What if your body were an ongoing source of joy and greatness? This book introduces you to the awareness that really is a different choice for you—and your sweet body.

Right Body for You

By Gary M. Douglas

This is a very different perspective about bodies and your ability to change yours. It might all be easier than you ever knew was possible! *Right Body for You* is a book that will inspire you and show you a different way of creating the body you truly desire.

Pragmatic Psychology:
Practical Tools For Being Crazy Happy

By Susanna Mittermaier

Everyone has at least one "crazy" person in their life, right (even if it's ourselves!)? And there are a lot of labels and diagnoses out there—depression, anxiety, ADD, ADHD, bi-polar, schizophrenia... What if there was a different possibility with mental illness—and what if change and happiness were a totally available reality? Susanna is a clinical psychologist with an amazing capacity to facilitate what this reality often defines as crazy from a totally different point of view—one of possibility and ease.

Divorceless Relationships

By Gary M. Douglas

Most of us spend a lot of time divorcing parts and pieces of ourselves in order to care for someone else. For example, you like to go jogging but instead of jogging, you spend that time with your partner to show him or her that you really care. "I love you so much that I would give up this thing that is valuable to me so I can be with you." This is one of the ways you divorce you to create an intimate relationship. How often does divorcing you really work in the long run?

CPSIA information can be obtained at www.ICGtesting.com
Printed in the USA
LVOW12s0000230514

386898LV00004B/15/P